NO ONE

DR JAMUNA PAI has spent the last twenty years being the one that A-list Bollywood stars, top industrialists and Miss Indias have turned to for their skin problems. She has also pioneered the skincare movement in this country, being the first to introduce many techniques to India including Botox, medi-facials, aesthetic peels as well as the Spanish brightening peel.

A doctor of medicine and surgery from the prestigious Nair Hospital and TNMC Medical, Dr Pai is one of India's leading medical cosmetologists who has been awarded the coveted Indira Gandhi Priyadarshini Award and the Bharat Gaurav Award for her excellent service in the field of skincare. Her chain of skincare clinics, Blush, was established in 1994 and – many clinics and franchises later – she continues to work with celebs, models and Miss Indias. She also trains doctors in aesthetic medicine at her training academy, DJPIMAC (Dr Jamuna Pai's Institute for Medical and Aesthetic Cosmetology).

She lives and works in Mumbai. This is her first book.

WHAT THE CELEBS SAY

'Dr Pai is a kind, knowledgeable and endearing person who, with her team at Blush, has made sure that I have no more acne today. She is the best.'

John Abraham, actor and producer

'Growing up, being a boy, I never felt the need to take much care of my skin. And even after becoming an actor, I still don't need to worry about it because Dr Pai makes sure she sorts me out always.'

Arjun Kapoor, actor

'The first time I met Dr Pai, I was struck by how stunning she looked! Dr Pai always makes me feel special, gives me her best advice and a hug! Every job is a portrait of the person who has done it and Dr Pai autographs hers with excellence.'

Juhi Chawla, actor, producer, entrepreneur, social activist, wife and mother

'I discovered Dr Pai's magical facials over ten years ago and since then I visit Blush for that extra dose of care and pampering that my skin needs. Dr Pai is extremely adept in her profession and I trust her implicitly. The entire Blush team also embodies the same values that she so strongly stands for: warmth, a steadfast work ethic and incomparable expertise.'

Gauri Khan

'Dr Pai is someone I have been trusting my skin with for the last twenty years. Her treatments are top-of-the-line and she uses the latest in technology. Thank you always.'

Malaika Arora Khan, actor, model and film producer

'Honestly, I don't believe in over use of products for my skin. I use a very light face wash twice daily; I drink copious quantities of water all through the day and really enjoy vegetable juices. I sleep as much as I can and make it a point to moisturize my face. And I'm pretty sure my workouts help to keep my skin glowing.'

Alia Bhatt, actor

'What amazes me is the consistency in quality and care that every single doctor [at Blush] provides. I'm glad that someone like Dr Pai took the initiative to understand the need for cosmetic clinics here in India.'

Vikram Phadnis, fashion designer and stylist

'I have a very hectic life and mostly in the public eye. The only person I trust with my skin is Dr Jamuna Pai. She is a magician.'

Rocky S., Creative Director for Rocky Star

'Being, as I am, pretty careless and lackadaisical about my skin, if at all I do receive the odd compliment about it, it's mostly due to Dr Jamuna Pai and her excellent staff at Blush.'

Malavika Sangghvi, columnist and poet

'It's her inner beauty that makes her so captivating on the outside as well. A beautiful face with an even more beautiful mind and soul. Thank you, Dr Pai, for all the tips on healthy living.'

Poonam Mahajan, MP and National Secretary, BJP

'I trust only Blush and the expert hands of Dr Jamuna Pai to look after my skin. After all, it's an investment towards looking good.'

Bhagyashree, actor

'Dr Pai's approach is holistic, stressing long-term well-being; she nurtures skin from the inside out, focusing not only on the right cleansing and moisturizing regimen but also on the food, sleep, vitamins and de-stressing each patient needs. Above all, Dr Pai has a great heart.'

Nandana Sen, actor and child rights activist

'Dr Pai has been my skin aesthetician since I was seventeen. When people ask me how I have such wonderful skin, even now I say that I owe it to Dr Pai.'

Alison Kanuga, event producer

'I have known Jamuna for almost ten years and apart from being one of my dearest friends, she also has the sole custody of the health of my skin. She has advised me on everything, from the smallest breakout to even the kind of make-up I should use. Month after month, since I first met Jamuna, I have been going for the most amazing facials and clean-ups to her clinic Blush.'

Mandira Bedi, actor, anchor and designer

'God has blessed me with a good complexion. However, for maintenance and regular nourishment from time to time, Blush is like a hidden treasure discovered and a boon to any woman who will discover it.'

Nagma, actor

'Jamuna is a wise and compassionate woman, who as a scientist is also on top of her science. A rare combination.'

Mallika Sarabhai, performer, choreographer and social activist

'If ever there was an angel sent from the Lord to look after my well-being, that angel is Jamuna Pai. JP stands for Just Perfect! Her discerning eye and magical hands perform miracles.'

Sabira Merchant, actor and corporate trainer

'Beauty with brains, Jamuna's in-depth and up-to-date knowledge of aesthetics blew my mind twenty years ago when I interviewed her for my fifty-two-episode TV show "Health Today". She went on to become my dearest friend and I rely upon her for her sensitive, caring ways but have yet to go to her for professional care. That's why I continue to age like an antique.'

Rashmi Uday Singh, TV show host and world gourmand; award-winning author of thirty-four books

'Dr Jamuna Pai looked after me and my fellow contestants during our pageant training days. She contributed significantly towards my final preparation for the Miss Asia Pacific World contest. The way she made me look enhanced my confidence and I won the crown straight away!'

Srishti Rana, Miss Asia Pacific World 2013

'My association with Dr Pai goes back to 2007 when I participated in Miss India South, where she was on the panel of experts. Apart from making sure I had the best skin, she has always been there as a source of support and motivation during Miss India and Miss World, support which continues till date.'

Parvathy Omanakuttan, actor and Miss World First Runner Up 2008

'One thing that has always touched me is [Dr Pai's] genuine concern to help every person who walks through her door. She is a gentle and sensitive person and someone I trust not just with my skin but as a person.'

Rajyalakshmi Rao, former Member-Judge, National Consumer Dispute Redressal Commission, and President, Indo-American Chamber of Commerce (WR)

'I was introduced to Dr Pai eleven years ago when I first arrived in Bombay. My fair skin had already been blighted with sun damage living in Australia and Los Angeles. Dr Pai not only helped stem further damage caused by the challenging Bombay climate, but reversed much of what had already happened. I would not trust my skin to anyone else.'

Samantha Nayar, businesswoman

'Jamuna-ji has changed the lives of many through her knowledge and compassion and I'm witness to it. I don't have words to thank her for her presence in my life.'

Sonu Nigam, singer

'Jamuna Pai has the rare gift of epitomizing the beauty she imparts to her clients. I've been consulting her for years, ever since I was a struggling actress. Her knowledge is so vast and her hand as light as air. She's a true maestro.'

Soni Razdan Bhatt, actor and director

'I can't thank Miss India enough for bringing this skin fairy into my life. My skin and I both feel the safest and happiest in Dr Pai's hands.'

Pooja Chopra, Miss India 2009

'Dr Pai's passion for cosmetology and commitment to giving her patients the best have been the main reasons for her success. And her expertise, knowledge and amazing aesthetic eye have transformed many a happy face.'

Rita Dhody, entrepreneur and fashion consultant

'Miss India Organization has been associated with Dr Jamuna Pai for around two decades as an esteemed panellist. Dr Pai is a perfectionist by nature, which always reflected in the results. She provides a tailor-made skincare routine for each girl, making all contestants feel special. MIO is extremely grateful to her for the association.'

Miss India Organization

'Having personally known her for twenty years, her inner beauty, grace and devotion to her late husband has always commanded my utmost respect and admiration. Her professional success can be fully attributed to her dedication, humility and thirst for knowledge that keeps her on top of all the trends in her industry. It's no surprise then that she's on the speed dial of divas, debutantes and domestic goddesses alike; after all, even Venus could do with Jamuna's magic touch!'

Pradeep Guha, Managing Director, 9X Media

'Dr Jamuna Pai is indeed the queen and pioneer of aesthetic beauty in India. Making heads turn for her looks as well as her warm, loving personal touch, I simply adore her and listen to her every whisper of advice.'

Marvie Ann Beck, Founder, Marvie Ann Beck Makeup and
Hair Academy

'Jamuna is the perfect face for Blush and the services it provides. She keeps herself updated with all the new techniques worldwide. I've enjoyed fabulous facials at the clinic.'

Arti Sarin, Head, PR and Corporate Communication, *Verve*

'Dr Jamuna Pai is a true pioneer and artist in the field of beauty, facial rejuvenation and anti-ageing. For over twenty years she has set the gold standard in India treating beautiful women and men. Besides her expertise as a medical practitioner, she is also an outstanding teacher of her technique to other doctors.'

Daniel C. Baker, MD, Professor of Plastic Surgery, New York University Medical School Institute of Reconstructive Plastic Surgery

'Dr Pai has years of experience and knowledge, so a friendly consultation helped in time to undo the damage of years of neglect and skin abuse! The Derma Peel is what I'd personally recommend with Dr Pai as I can see good results with it and the quarterly follow up guarantees results!'

Terence Lewis, TV show judge, choreographer and artist

'Dr Jamuna Pai deserves to be called the pioneer in the field of Aesthethics in India; she started the whole aesthetic movement when no one else did. I would consider her a mentor in aesthetic and cosmetic work.'

Dr Srilata Trasi, dermato-surgeon, cosmetologist and laser consultant

'Dr Pai's understanding of my skin keeps me looking healthy and stress free. She is awesome!'

Shazahn Padamsee, actor

'Doc is a master of her art. I have seen her transform faces and change people's lives. She is a true miracle performer.'

Marc Robinson, beauty pageant and fashion director; choreographer

NO ONE HAS TO KNOW

SMART ANTI-AGEING FOR INDIAN SKIN

Dearest
Lymaraina,

DR JAMUNA PAI

With
Gayatri Pahlajani

Love & regards.

Jamuna
..

Collins

MUMBAI   08·02·2018

First published in India in 2015 by Collins
An imprint of HarperCollins *Publishers*

P-ISBN: 978-93-5136-458-0
E-ISBN: 978-93-5136-459-7

2 4 6 8 10 9 7 5 3

HarperCollins *Publishers*
A-75, Sector 57, Noida, Uttar Pradesh 201301, India
1 London Bridge Street, London, SE1 9GF, United Kingdom
Hazelton Lanes, 55 Avenue Road, Suite 2900, Toronto, Ontario M5R 3L2
and 1995 Markham Road, Scarborough, Ontario M1B 5M8, Canada
25 Ryde Road, Pymble, Sydney, NSW 2073, Australia
195 Broadway, New York, NY 10007, USA

Typeset in 11/15 Mercury Display
by Jojy Philip, New Delhi

Printed and bound at
Thomson Press (India) Ltd.

To my late husband, Dr Bhasker Pai, my strength, my support

I love you more than you know

I miss you more than you know

Contents

Preface

Of Beauty and Beautification

Archaeologists excavating the ancient Indus Valley civilization in the 1920s didn't just discover its brick houses and sophisticated plumbing systems. As dirt yielded to the demands of discovery, they began to uncover jewellery. And a lot of it. An ancient Harappan was found buried with a necklace of 300 soapstone beads. Other evidence suggested that both men and women bedecked themselves with earrings, ear studs, amulets and bangles. You could almost picture giggling girls trying on arm-bangles as they styled their hair in elaborate hairstyles.[1]

As early as about 5000 years ago, we wanted to look good.

Beautification is not a modern construct. From the beginning of society as we know it, men and women have been captivated by their own image. Before the discovery

---

[1] 'Primary History: Land of the Indus', accessed 30 December 2014, http://www.bbc.co.uk/schools/primaryhistory/indus_valley/.

of the mirror, human beings would see their faces in dark pools of water or pieces of polished glass or stone. Carvings on the walls of Egyptian tombs and Indian temples suggest that ancient people put thought and care into their outward appearance. Queen Cleopatra (c.69–30 BC) is believed to have bathed in ass's milk (the lactic acid in milk is an alpha hydroxy acid that is used in chemical peels today; she was clearly on to something). Lead was used in many cultures – with devastating side effects – to beautify eyes and even faces. Evidence of evolving civilizations has, in so many cases, existed side by side with evidence of beautification suggesting that, like war and learning and religion, beautification was also a priority. And this was before television, beauty pageants, fillers and Botox.[2]

As a medical practitioner prescribing both medical and cosmetic cures for skin and hair conditions over the last twenty years for tens of thousands of clients, I have seen how skin problems can negatively affect the psyche and how clear, glowing skin can restore confidence. Skin – especially of the face – is usually the first thing you notice about someone. To dismiss the psychological impact of skin problems as pigments of our imagination or as manifestations of our vanity is to undermine what is perhaps a very primal need to be and look attractive.

Our standards have definitely changed, though. And so have the client profiles that I treat: everyone's now looking to tone down the wrinkles, tone down the grey and stay in shape. And while being slimmer is not necessarily better,

---

[2] Botox is the trade name for botunilum toxin, a neuromodulator, used in anti-ageing treatments.

I do believe that beautification and outward appearance is about discovering and maintaining a standard that you think is right for *you*. A girl who doesn't want to wax her legs may be fussy about the shape of her eyebrows. A man who thinks pedicures are a bit too girly for him may spend half his salary on hair products. Immaculate eyebrows is her standard. Immaculate hair is his. I also believe that beautification is about guilt or rather, the lack of it, and whether you feel that it is all right to take time out for yourself to keep yourself glowing.

I've been guiltless about prioritizing beautification since I was about ten. I was your garden-variety class topper, on track to becoming a doctor. But as the school's headgirl, I used to monitor class as closely as I monitored the ironing of the box pleats on my blue uniform. I used to enlist the help of my long-suffering maid to pluck my eyebrows and wax my legs with a recipe I only brought out when my parents went out. And I would spend most of my allowance on haircuts. I made a commitment – very early on – to maintain *my* standard.

Later, married to the love of my life and with two boys, as a full-fledged doctor with the Brihanmumbai Municipal Corporation (BMC), I was still dissatisfied despite being a hands-on, working mother because I was unable to fully commit to my passion for beautification. But a chance meeting with a qualified doctor, who also did facials, gave me my Eureka moment: why not combine my medical knowledge with the art and science of beautification? At that time, dermatologists treated acne but not the scars, while beauticians treated the scars but not the recurring episodes of acne. And so, in 1994, Blush Clinics was born. And with it, my second life.

But with birth comes the pain of labour. In the nineties, nobody else was working in this field. There were no protocols or rules for treating Indian skin. I was already an MBBS but there were no reputed cosmetology schools in India back then; I came back from training in beautification from the UK with the equipment and the materials. But all anyone was taught at the time abroad was how to conduct these procedures on Caucasian or white skin. Indian skin has its own peculiarities, Indian climate its own impact. What would the start-to-finish procedure be for treating acne and acne scars in Indians? Or pigmentation patches? Or laser hair removal? We didn't know. And we needed to have our own set of rules.

It didn't help that, twenty years ago, India was not on the radar for international brands. There were no distributors for lasers or Botox, which started three years *after* I first brought it to India in the year 2000. The first laser machine I was swayed into buying did nothing for acne scars on melanin-rich Indian skin. Through trial and error, through testing and re-testing, through adjusting settings and dosages, I had to make my own rules and, sometimes, break them in order to find the best solutions for Indian skin. I did that by trying out every single procedure on myself first. It's something I still do.

But beautification is not always about injections or jars or tubes. It is also about what's there in our backyards, on our kitchen shelves or in our grandmother's recipe books. It's sometimes about what is *not* written in the rulebooks but passed down through the generations with love and care. Indians discovered the gem that is turmeric way before the Western world did. And scientific experiments continue to prove us right. This book will help you find the right balance between natural, homemade remedies and more elaborate cosmetic procedures. Because something that may work for you may not be right for someone else.

More importantly, this book will also help you enhance what you have been already blessed with. And hopefully it will help you appreciate just how beautiful you already are. We'll cover the hottest beautification trends and celeb secrets, whether it is just simple maintenance or more elaborate procedures, whether you're just looking to scrub your face clean or you'd like advice to get fillers done. Be confident with *your* standard. Not everyone's standard does – or should – fit yours.

Your face tells the world the journey you have travelled. To that end, the best form of beautification shows a life beautifully lived. On the other hand, beautification done badly erases the life that you have lived and why would you want that? Lastly, this book will help you find that oh-so-delicate balance between enhancement and transformation and between transformation and *mutation*. For the last twenty years, my team of doctors and I have been working to perfect the 'less is more' approach to beautification. Because the best form of anti-ageing is when you or people around you notice that there *is* a difference but can't seem to figure out what it is. Because the best form of anti-ageing is the kind that keeps you – and the people around you – guessing. No One Has to Know.

Not everyone will find their way to my clinics. But I think that reading this book will help develop confidence and good health, something I wish for every human being. And do note that in all of the above, I do not use the word 'beauty' but 'beautification'. There's a difference. Because while I hope I can help beautify you, I believe that true beauty is inherent to you, your thoughts and your actions. No matter what your standard may be.

1

The Ageing Continuum

From the moment you are a little twinkle in someone's eye to the moment you are a little twinkle in the sky, you are ageing. Skin, just like all other organs, degenerates over the years from birth to death. It is a biological certainty and needs to be embraced. While this may sound odd coming from a cosmetologist, it is actually the key to understanding that even *anti*-ageing needs to be approached with wisdom, balance and self-love. Before I get into the jars, bottles, packs and more that put up an impressive fight against ageing, it is important to first understand skin better as an organ, how it works and how it ages. Because in order to repair something, you first need to know how it broke. To get over your skin problems, you first need to get under it.

Before crying over those sun spots and fine lines, you must understand the beauty and wonder of your skin and what it does – and has been doing – to protect your body. The skin is the largest organ of the human body and not only defines the way you look on the *outside* but is also a pretty good indication of how your body is doing on the *inside*. It offers two layers of protection:

1

The Epidermis
The Dermis

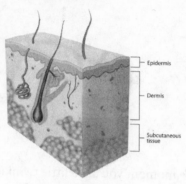

Skin: A Cross-section

THE EPIDERMIS

The epidermis is the topmost layer of your skin and consists of 15-20 layers of dead skin cells. These layers are all that stand between you and the outside world. Its job is to protect you from the sun, water and harmful external substances. It is also that layer that gives you the feeling of 'touch'. For the purposes of this book, the two main sub-layers of the epidermis that we need to understand are: The stratum corneum and the melanin (in the basal layer).

The Raincoat | Stratum Corneum

STRATUM CORNEUM

The job of waterproofing is done by the stratum corneum, your body's raincoat, which is also the topmost layer of the epidermis. This 'raincoat' consists of tightly grouped cells that protect your body, waterproofing it *and* retaining moisture all at the same time: the stratum corneum keeps water out of your body so that your internal organs are protected from bacteria and germs but also traps enough water so that your skin looks dewy, fresh and hydrated. So you can go and play in the rain or swim in the ocean, get wet on the outside but stay dry on the inside.

It is also the most visible part of your body and the skin you see on your face, your hands, arms, body is all stratum corneum. This is the layer of skin that you cleanse, exfoliate, moisturize and apply sunscreen and ointments on, and has its own way of ageing and, therefore, *anti*-ageing.

MELANIN

Here's a familiar enough scenario: After a soul-satisfying afternoon shopping trip, you're out in the hot sun trying to catch a cab back home. But no cabbie wants to take you and armed with so many bags, the bus is the last thing you want to take. By the time you finally reach home, your arms, face or feet or other uncovered parts are darker than the rest of your body. Along with your shopping, you've brought home a tan.

You may be upset. Don't be. This just means that melanin has done its job. Just as the stratum cornuem is your body's natural raincoat, the melanin is your body's natural 'suncoat'. The melanin pigment sits in the lowest

The Suncoat | Melanin

sub-layer of the epidermis and shields your body from the extremely harmful effects of the sun, or rather, the sun's ultraviolet (UV) rays.

When you tan, it is actually the result of the fierce battle that melanin has just fought with its arch enemy, the sun. And the fact that you have tanned – and not burned – means that melanin has *won* the battle. A tan is melanin's way of protecting you from ageing. And here's how: before the sun's rays reach the collagen layers in your *dermis* (collagen is in charge of how your skin wrinkles), it is intercepted by the melanin in the *epidermis*, which acts like a true warrior, absorbing the sun's rays before it can cause any further damage to your skin. The absorption causes your skin to turn darker. Without melanin, however, the sun will cheerfully go straight to the dermis and, over time, dent your collagen layer, causing premature lines and wrinkles.

This doesn't mean that we don't need additional protection from the sun in the form of sunscreens and sunblocks; melanin can only protect us that much. But the more melanin we have, the slower we age. And the more melanin we have, the darker our skin tone.

Herein lies the problem. So many of us are dissatisfied with our skin colour. So many matrimonial ads want 'fair' brides. So many ads show the fairer girl landing the job, winning the prize, or getting the guy. Barkha Dutt, Group Editor of NDTV, recently invited me to a TV show with Nandita Das to discuss whether 'dark is beautiful'. While I eventually couldn't manage to make it to the show, I agreed wholeheartedly with Nandita that as long as the colour and tone are even, brown skin is a beautiful asset and as sensual as fair skin. At Blush, we do carry out skin brightening treatments but we do this more to even out patchy pigmentation and give the skin a seamless colour tone rather than lightening someone's complexion.

While the Indian psyche is still preoccupied with fairness, what we don't realize is that we are often unhappy with the one thing that not only protects us from diseases like cancer, but also keeps us looking younger. There is a far higher incidence of skin cancer among Caucasian or whiter skin tones as opposed to our skin tones or darker. And yet, this is what so many of us want to change about ourselves: our beautiful brown.

THE DERMIS

The second layer of the skin – dermis or 'true skin' – supports the epidermis and is thick and durable. The dermis regulates body temperature through the two-step process of sweat and evaporation – your skin has about 2.5 *million* sweat glands on its surface – and, as this layer of skin consists of oil glands, it also helps regulate the secretion of oils both on your skin and hair. *The thicker the dermis, the plumper your skin, the younger you look.* This layer of skin is mainly made up of The Big C – Collagen.

The Thermostat | The Dermis

Collagen is what gives skin its durability and resilience and is responsible for when and how we wrinkle. When it's damaged or dented, we get wrinkles and lines. The sun dents collagen, ageing dents collagen, our lifestyle dents collagen, repeated motions like smiling or frowning over time dent collagen.
Even if you've never stepped out in the sun, never smoked, never drank, never smiled, never laughed, never frowned or squinted, collagen could get dented through the internal chemical process of oxidation going on inside your body, which is partly because of what you eat. Which is why it is recommended that you eat and drink foods high in antioxidants: to combat oxidation, and therefore, ageing.

The Rubberband | Collagen

Treat your skin badly and collagen will dent faster, playing spoilsport sooner than your genes will. And it's not just wrinkles. Within collagen is also a fibre called elastin, which works the same way as a well-fitted glove does. Over time, a well-fitted glove loses its elasticity and doesn't fit as well. Over time, the elastin fibres lose their elasticity and that's why the skin doesn't cover our body as well as it used to. It becomes less elastic, less snug, more ill-fitting and then it begins to hang on us.

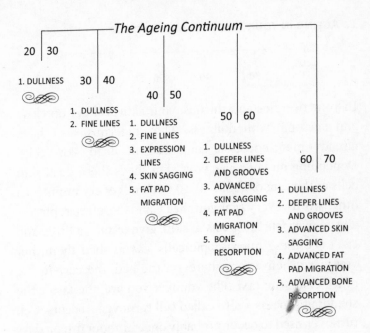

The Ageing Continuum

20 | 30

1. DULLNESS

           30 | 40

       1. DULLNESS
       2. FINE LINES

                40 | 50

               1. DULLNESS
               2. FINE LINES
               3. EXPRESSION
                   LINES
               4. SKIN SAGGING
               5. FAT PAD
                   MIGRATION

                       50 | 60

                     1. DULLNESS
                     2. DEEPER LINES
                        AND GROOVES
                     3. ADVANCED
                        SKIN SAGGING
                     4. FAT PAD
                        MIGRATION
                     5. BONE
                        RESORPTION

                              60 | 70

                             1. DULLNESS
                             2. DEEPER LINES
                                AND GROOVES
                             3. ADVANCED SKIN
                                SAGGING
                             4. ADVANCED FAT
                                PAD MIGRATION
                             5. ADVANCED BONE
                                RESORPTION

THE AGEING CONTINUUM

So how do we age? Ageing is part genetics; it's what we were born with. But a large part of how we look has to do with what we **do** to our skin. Before we get into that, though, I've first mapped out the Ageing Continuum for all of us irrespective of our genes.

Depending on your lifestyle, your skincare habits, genetic make-up and hormonal changes, ageing doesn't always happen in this sequence but it's more or less the same. For example, the processes of bone resorption and fat pad migration (which will be explained later in the chapter) have been mapped as per age only when it starts to look the most *apparent* on your face – the ageing process could start earlier than they appear.

1. AGEING IN YOUR TWENTIES AND THIRTIES

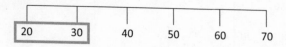

In your twenties and thirties, your skin will get up close and personal with dullness. The epidermis, as I have already mentioned, is composed of dead skin cells. Depending on your age, your skin sheds these dead skin cells at the rate of about 30-40,000 cells every minute. In other words, every year you shed – and therefore replace – a little over *four kilograms* of skin, give or take a little. You can't see these microscopic cells as you shed them, but you leave them everywhere: on the bed, the carpet, the office chair, the taxi. The younger you are, the faster the shedding process – also called cell turnover – occurs. Cell turnover used to occur probably once in about fifteen days when you were younger, but the older you get, the longer it takes. In your fifties, cell turnover probably takes place once in about fifty days. In other words, as your body slows down, so does your cell renewal cycle. Slowdown can start as early as your mid-twenties.

Cell renewal is crucial because the new layer of skin – especially the topmost stratum corneum – is the layer that is most visible to the world. When cells are not renewed quickly, the wrinkles, the sunburn, the blotches are slower to fade and makes the skin look older and duller as you lose that 'glow'. Additionally, when millions and millions of unshed dead cells collect, the epidermis cannot do its job of protecting all that well – that's the whole point of exfoliation: to shed dead skin cells and keep the skin looking young, tight and supple.

2. AGEING IN YOUR THIRTIES AND FORTIES

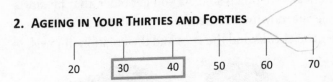

Collagen and elastin start to have their hissy fits and begin breaking down and denting in our thirties and forties because of various reasons including, as we had discussed, sun damage, repetitive facial expressions and oxidative stress. In your thirties and forties, therefore, you will see fine lines appearing on your face. As you grow older, these lines and wrinkles will deepen into grooves.

Collagen breakdown could also be because of whether or not you exercise. Collagen dents when blood supply to the skin decreases as you get older. Fresh blood brings with it nutrients that nourish collagen; lack of blood supply leads to wrinkles. Increased activity from physical exercise ensures that blood rushes to the collagen layer, and that's why the Fifth E of this book is Exercise.

3. AGEING IN YOUR FORTIES AND FIFTIES

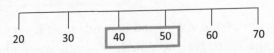

In the forties and fifties, there is a noticeable loss of fat on the face. Fat loss on the rest of your body mostly makes you look younger. Fat loss on your face, however, mostly makes you look *older*. There is superficial and deep fat on your face – for example, on your cheeks, which is what makes your cheeks so 'pinch'able. As you get older, that fat starts to migrate downwards, leading to hollowing of the face under the cheeks and the eyes and the creation of jowls.

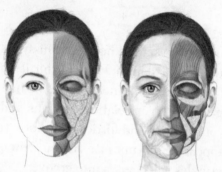

Take a look at the difference in both skin and fat over time. In the second image on the right, the fat has migrated south, which is evident in the development of jowls and sagging cheeks. Gravity also pitches in here, adding to the downward slide.

4. AGEING IN YOUR FIFTIES AND SIXTIES AND OVER

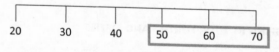

In your fifties and sixties and beyond, apart from fat pad migration, there is noticeable loss of one more element that defines both your face and your body: the bone. Bone resorbs over time, especially from age fifty onwards.

To give you a clearer idea of what I mean, look at the image on the right. Not only have the muscles thinned out,

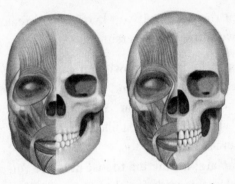

but the eye sockets are larger, the nasal bone has receded, the jaw (or mandible) has become smaller and the apples of the cheek (the highest point in the cheekbone) have also resorbed, which is why they look much flatter. The temporal bone has also receded, creating hollows on either side of the forehead. Also consistent with advanced ageing is the thinning of the intervertebral discs in the seventies, resulting in height shrinkage. Case in point: my ninety-three-year-old mother-in-law is shorter than she used be and, consequently, she has to tuck in her saris further when she gets ready.

SO NOW WHAT?

All's not lost. The best thing about knowing about the ageing process is that you are aware of the finale of this particular movie no matter at what stage you are in. If you're reading this book at the age of thirty-two, you know that your collagen is beginning to break down and you need to take steps to delay it. If you're in your late forties or fifties, you know that the fat has migrated or will start to. But whatever age you are, there are things you can do to combat the ageing. If you know what breaks it down, you can work towards reversing it.

Is your skin losing its glow? You can recover this with manual exfoliation, peels and microdermabrasion.

Is your facial skin losing fat? You can combat this – if you want to – with the help of fat fillers or hyaluronic acid fillers. Facial exercises can help too.

Is your facial skin starting to lose muscle? You can, again, try to delay this with facial exercises. And regular, full-body exercises.

Is your skin starting to wrinkle? You can delay *and reverse* collagen breakdown by eating right and exercising, by applying sunblock, by taking daily care of your skin and by using night repair creams. You can address deeper lines and grooves – if you like – through fillers and medical procedures like Botox.

Is your skin losing elasticity? You can make the skin thicker and tighter with the help of radiofrequency or chemical peels.

Is your bone starting to resorb? While nothing significant can be done to reverse this process, you can start taking nutritional supplements as well as train with weights and pay better attention to bone health.

The important thing to remember here is to *never underestimate the value of prevention*. Symptoms of ageing can be controlled even before they start. And the earlier we start, the faster we delay and, in some cases, the faster we reverse. You will also find that so many skincare solutions are commonsensical ones or things that are good for your overall health. But some – especially for fat pad migration, where fillers help the most – are really up to you. It is about your own sense of identity and the standard you see yourself maintaining. All I want to emphasize here is that no matter where you currently belong on the Ageing Continuum, a lot can still be done to turn back time.

It is never too late.

THE ACID TEST

It's the king of all snap tests: the pH test. This will tell you immediately how healthy both your skin and body are. While not designed to replace other measures of health assessment, the pH test is a pretty good indicator. The pH or potential of Hydrogen is the concentration of the Hydrogen ion in the body. pH levels are measured for different tissues in the body and range from 1-14. If the pH level is 0-7, then it means that the tissue is acidic; if it's over 7, then it is alkaline. 7, of course, is neutral. While most other body tissues need to be more alkaline than acidic, *skin has to be more acidic than alkaline*.

And here's why. The acidity of skin protects us from a whole gamut of diseases and puts up a fight against the outside world on behalf of our internal organs. Which is why it is also called the Acid Mantle. If the acidity levels of the skin are too low, it's vulnerable to bacterial attack. Too high, and the skin becomes too dry. 5.5 is the optimum pH level for the skin. Which is why choosing soaps and cleansers should be done with care. Soaps are mostly alkaline. If the soap has too much detergent – which means it is very alkaline – it can strip the skin of its acidity, upsetting the pH balance, making the skin more prone to pimples and rashes. Not to mention, disease.

2

What Speeds Up Ageing

Because you're only as young as your lifestyle

Skin is a tattletale. It usually tells people things you don't always want them to know. It could tell your clients that you pulled an all-nighter on the presentation you are making before them. It could tell your spouse that the fight you had kept you up all night. It could tell a trained dermatologist or cosmetologist that you have dandruff without them even checking your scalp. Skin also tattles on the life you are leading: a smoker has a lot more pigmentation or patchy skin, and is more wrinkled than say his or her own brother or sister from the same gene pool. No one gossips more than your skin. You can keep it quiet with make-up sometimes, but that's neither a smart answer nor a long-term one.

Skin also reflects your inner turmoil – your PCOS, your hormones, your stress levels. Having treated thousands of clients over the last twenty years, I now feel that I can

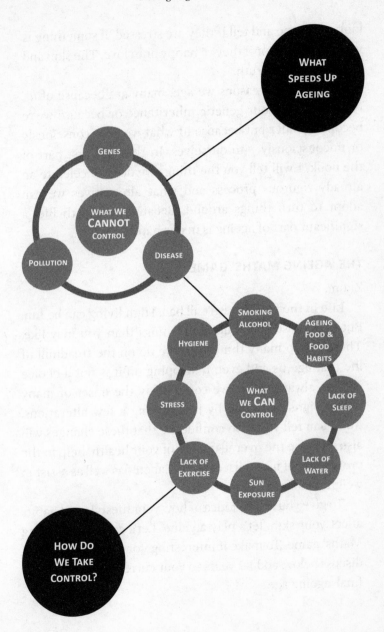

WHAT
SPEEDS UP
AGEING

GENES

WHAT WE
CANNOT
CONTROL

POLLUTION

DISEASE

SMOKING
ALCOHOL

HYGIENE

AGEING
FOOD &
FOOD
HABITS

STRESS

WHAT
WE CAN
CONTROL

LACK OF
SLEEP

LACK OF
EXERCISE

SUN
EXPOSURE

LACK OF
WATER

HOW DO
WE TAKE
CONTROL?

look at anyone and tell if they are stressed, if something is worrying them, or if they're happy or in love. The skin and the eyes radiate truth.

Of the many reasons we age, many are because of *us*. Not because of our genetic inheritance or because we're becoming older but because of what we do – consciously or unconsciously – to ourselves. In this, the first part of the book, I will tell you the things we do to accelerate an already rigorous process and what alternatives we can adopt to turn things around. Because, like with life, a significant part of ageing is in our hands.

THE 'AGEING MATHS' GAME

Zoom.

Life in the fast lane isn't all bad. High living can be fun. But it can also speed up more things than you may like. There are so many things that we do on the treadmill of life that age us and even if stepping off it is not a choice we can always make, we could delay the onset of many visible signs of ageing by just making a few alterations. And I can tell you with confidence that these changes will also increase the overall quality of your health, help in the prevention of heart disease and diabetes as well as assist in weight management.

To give you a better idea of how your lifestyle and habits affect your skin, let's play a game. Let's call it the 'Ageing Maths' game. To make it interesting, for every point that I discuss below, add 1-2 years to your current age to get your final 'ageing age'.

PHOTOAGEING

Ageing due to overexposure to the sun – or photoageing – is one of the most preventable forms of ageing. As we know, the sun penetrates our skin and damages the collagen, which is responsible for wrinkles. Melanin swoops in and absorbs the harmful UV rays, protecting us but also tanning us in the process.

But there is only so much melanin can do to protect collagen breakdown. Visible photoageing signs include age spots, thickened skin (due to dead skin build up) and deep wrinkles, ageing us far beyond our chronological years. You will always find people with heavy outdoorsy lives or those who are very fair skinned or those who live in tropical countries or near the sea, sand or at higher altitudes ageing faster (the last is because of the deflected rays of the sun).

Even the skin on our face, hands and feet age faster than the rest of our bodies. The truest test of this is if you compare, for example, your mother's skin on the exposed parts of her body, like the face, neck, hands and feet, to the unexposed parts like the thighs and the upper arms. You will be amazed that the unexposed skin looks much younger than the exposed skin. That's how potent sun damage is.

Yet, we step out in the sun, unprotected, every other day. It takes little to invest in a good-quality sunscreen and not more than a minute to put it on. While we will get into this in greater detail in the chapter **Everyday**, do remember, this is *the* most preventable thing we can do.

Do you wear sunscreen everyday?
If not, add two years to your age.

STRESS

Stress is hard to quantify or control. We're all stressed at some point or the other; it is part of the human condition. As I'm writing this book, I have clients in the waiting room, a phone that never sleeps, two doctors queuing up to ask about something urgent and a mountain of unanswered emails.

However, in this context, when I talk about stress that ages you, I am referring to prolonged, chronic stress. Chronic stress is the culprit for multiple skin problems that include psoriasis, hives, acne and thinning of the skin. When you are stressed over a protracted period of time, the process of skin renewal slows to a crawl and you start looking ashen and dull. And when the renewal slows down, you are more vulnerable to wrinkles.

Prolonged stress also causes oxidative stress. To understand what oxidative stress is, do note that oxidation is all around you. You see it when a fruit turns brown or begins to rot when exposed to the air or when silver starts to turn black. To put it simply, oxygen is a highly reactive element and is a bit of a sword with two edges. On the one hand, it's the giver of life, the air we breathe. On the other hand, the process of oxidation can be destructive, as unstable as it is unpredictable. The very same process that rots fruit also takes place inside our body with more dangerous consequences: oxidation releases 'free radicals' that slowly damage organs to include the skin and have also been linked to cancer. Oxidative stress dents collagen. Dented collagen leads to wrinkles. It's the same old story.

This kind of stress also elevates levels of cortisol – the stress hormone – which increases our blood sugar levels. Excess sugar, apart from weight gain and heart problems, also compromises collagen. Highly stressed people tend to drink more alcohol, have bad eating habits and exercise less, all of which lead to ageing.

But, like I said, being relatively stress-free is extremely hard to implement. For stress is our way of reacting to the environment. It's how we take on the world around us. Ideally, we need to take active steps to change our attitude as well as work smarter to get through our day with ease. I'll tell you what works for me: firstly, delegation. To counter the stress I face on a daily basis, I have allowed people around me to take on more responsibility. I have also set aside some 'Me Time' when I meet my friends, play with my grandson and do things that I like, which sometimes can mean doing nothing at all for a little time every day and on the weekend.

I advise my clients to do fun things that release the 'happy hormones'. The hormones endorphin, dopamine and serotonin are released via exercise. I also usually recommend relaxation activities like gardening, shopping or listening to music. Being happy will make you radiant, both from the inside and out.

And, lastly, whether you are going through a painful divorce or facing the loss of your job, please remember you're not alone. Everyone has got something they have to deal with even if their life seems perfect from the outside. Keep staying, thinking and being positive because good always follows the bad. Focus on achieving goals. After you reach one, move on to the next. Stay happy and true to yourself. It is only then you can be the best you can be.

 Does heavy stress take over your life?
If yes, add two years to your age.

AGEING FOODS

Certain foods age you. Fast foods, aerated drinks, processed foods, foods with trans fats and hydrogenated oils, refined flour, artificial sweeteners, teas, coffees, red meat and foods high in sugar and salt (sodium) release free radicals causing oxidative stress. It's tricky to exactly figure out which foods age us because so many foods have these in smaller or larger quantities and we eat them without knowing their compositions. That is why I have an entire chapter, **Eat**, devoted to ageing and anti-ageing foods.

 Do you think you have been eating 'ageing' foods?
If yes, add one year to your age.

LACK OF SLEEP

Sleep is the time when the skin repairs itself. That's why it's often called 'beauty sleep'. We've addressed this again in detail in **Everyday**, but for now, if you aren't getting enough sleep, you should be concerned.

 Do you get enough sleep?
If not, add one year to your age.

LACK OF WATER

Are you dehydrated? All your organs need water, and not just the skin. When skin cells don't get enough water, the skin turns dry and dry skin is more wrinkle-prone than nourished, hydrated skin. Again, **Everyday** will discuss this in greater detail but for now, if you aren't getting enough water, add a year to your age.

+1 **Are you drinking enough water?**
If not, add one year to your age.

ALCOHOL

Alcohol is not only high in sugar, it aids in the release of free radicals, which age you. It also dehydrates you, which again accelerates ageing.

+1 **Are you a heavy drinker?**
If so, add one year to your age.

LACK OF EXERCISE

When you exercise, the process of oxygenation (which is different from oxidation) helps the skin to regenerate collagen. Lack of exercise ages the skin. We've addressed this in greater detail in **Exercise**.

+1 **Do you exercise?**
If not, add a year to your age.

LACK OF HYGIENE

Are you taking care of your skin like washing your face twice a day? Are you exfoliating on a regular basis, doing your facials? Yes men, even you. Is your stratum corneum overloaded with dead skin cells? Do you have a night repair routine? No? Then we have lots to discuss in **Everyday.**

+1 **Do you take care of your skin on a daily basis, both at night and during the day?**
If not, add one year to your age.

SMOKING

Apart from *not* using sunscreen, smoking is one of the worst things you can do to yourself. To understand this is to understand the role of Vitamin C in maintaining your health. Vitamin C is an antioxidant, which is also a free radical scavenger, that is, it flushes out the harmful free radicals out of your body. Every single cigarette you smoke depletes Vitamin C from your body. And not only that, it further *adds* more free radicals. Also, the repetitive movements of your mouth while smoking dent collagen over time, causing lines and wrinkles. Lastly, smoker's skin takes on a sallow appearance due to the chemicals overloading the liver.

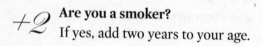

+2 **Are you a smoker?**
If yes, add two years to your age.

YOUR 'AGEING AGE'

To find out your 'ageing age', add your actual age (A) to the additional years you have added for every habit that ages you (B) mentioned earlier.

So how old are you really?

Needless to say, lifestyle-related ageing does not happen always in this precise, mathematical manner. And even if it did, your genes will come into play even if you are guilty of all the things above. So if you're forty-five and have an ageing lifestyle and feel you still look your age when you look in the mirror, you're right. The point of the Ageing Maths game is to simply warn you to never underestimate the impact of your lifestyle on the ageing process. Even if lifestyle does not impact the way you age now, it's possible that it will at some point in your life. Because I've seen many examples of it in my clinic.

I've seen it when clients walk in after a tremendous life-changing event like the sudden death of a loved one, they seem to have aged overnight because of the stress and sadness. I've seen it when clients walk in after having recovered from eating disorders with sunken eyes that belie their age. I can also tell the ones who are out in the sun all the time without protection. And I can tell which client is a heavy drinker and smoker and has not been eating right. Sometimes I guess their ages right, and sometimes I have been off by 5-10 years; they look so much older than they actually are. Like I said, the skin radiates truth.

Of course, it's not just the lifestyle; you can't underestimate the role of hormones and disease in the way you age. Even if you are eating right and doing everything else right, there could be underlying hormonal problems, and I will address that in later chapters. You can't underestimate the impact of genes either. Your genetic factors dictate the rate at which your ageing process progresses. Take a look at your parents' skin to see how you will age; I have seen young adults in their twenties with deep laugh lines because it's a family trait.

I've also seen lifestyle-related ageing reverse beautifully. Photoageing damage can be reversed with better care and improved hydration that slow down the march of time. I've seen clients who have reorganized their lives looking so much happier and so much *younger*. Better sleeping habits, better hygiene, more dietary care, reduction in stress, more exercise and quitting smoking can turn back the clock subtly and effectively and affect your overall health. Because when you adjust your lifestyle, it's anti-ageing for every single part of your body. Not just the skin.

3

No One Has to Know

I could have named my book anything, really; I had twenty years' worth of titles swimming around in my head. But why *this* particular title? Why 'No One Has to Know'? Why shouldn't anyone know? Am I perpetuating the culture of silence that surrounds Botox or peels or facials? Am I encouraging some sort of cloak-and-dagger approach to beautification? Am I saying that getting beautified is something to be ashamed of?

I'm saying none of these things.

Over the last two decades, I've found that the best and most glorious way to *anti*-age is if you look the best and most glorious version of *you*. Where no one can exactly put a finger as to why you look so much younger and radiant but also know that this is *you* at your most beautiful and not a plastic, unnatural shadow of your former self. *No One Has to Know* is the Bible for the subtle and delicate anti-ageing practices and techniques that my team and I have practised over the last two decades. The core principle that underlines my approach is 'Less Is More' and I'm debuting my 5E approach to skincare with the hope that it will benefit you as much as it has benefited me. My 5 Es of absolute essential skincare:

1. **E**veryday. The first 'E', Everyday, the longest chapter in the book, will detail daily regimens for anti-ageing skincare to include morning care, day care and night care as well as a buying guide for selecting the right products depending on your budget. Embrace the subtle but definitive transformation that daily habits bring to your face.

2. **E**xfoliate. The second 'E', Exfoliate, will highlight one of the most fundamental lessons of skincare, beautifully and gently revealing the best layers of your skin by removing the unwanted top layers.

3. **E**rase. The third 'E', Erase, will identify common skin problems – acne, pigmentation and deeper grooves and wrinkles – and show how to reduce them in an effective, gentle manner.

4. **E**at. The fourth 'E', Eat, will identify the best anti-ageing food practices that would work not only for your skin but also for the rest of your body.

5. **E**xercise. The final 'E', Exercise, will outline both the need for general exercise as well as present some easy facial exercises to gently delay ageing.

Please note that all solutions prescribed by me in this book are non-surgical procedures. When I mean *non-surgical*, I mean anything that can be in the form of creams, lotions, facials, equipment like microdermabrasion wands, lasers and skin tighteners and even injectibles like Botox, fillers and the like. On the other hand, *surgical techniques*, performed by cosmetic or plastic surgeons, are more invasive interventions to make more drastic or permanent changes. Surgical anti-ageing or cosmetic techniques are touched upon in the chapter *Excise* (not part of the 5E approach), if that is something you are interested in. My intention is to provide as much information as possible. What you want to take from this book is really up to *you*.

Just a few words of caution, though: if you're reading this and are pregnant or planning a baby or breastfeeding or under any medication, please check with your doctor before attempting any of the solutions as some are contraindicated for pregnancy and lactation, and even supplements should not be taken without the consent of your gynaecologist. The same goes for problem skin or sensitive skin or skin under treatment: please consult your doctor before taking the next steps in this book. Do also note that the solutions discussed here are meant for the face, unless otherwise specified.

Each of the 5Es will detail what needs to be done but for your convenience, I've included beauty calendars as per your decade – skincare for your twenties, thirties, forties and so on at the end of the book. So no matter what your age may be at the time of reading this book, you have a schedule for skincare designed for your age band all set to be implemented immediately. I've also included solutions that work for different price bands, are easily available and work well for the Indian skin and climate.

The 5E approach, when done all together will, I believe, transform your face without making a caricature of it, and enhance your features without exaggerating them. Some of the procedures in the third E, Erase, are optional but it's really, like I said, up to the standard you see maintaining for yourself. And what means beautiful to you.

Did you know that the way you take care of your skin on a daily basis could turn back the clock *one day at a time*? Did you know that solutions for everyday skincare lie on your kitchen shelves? **Everyday** is a detailed plan for daily skincare zeroing in on the basic minimum that your skin needs to feed on from day to night.

The First 'E'. Everyday.
Because you are only as young as your Everyday care.

One of the easiest and most effective things you can do for anti-ageing is to have a daily routine for day and night care of your skin. Since the skin slowly ages every second of every day of your life, a daily routine keeps ageing in check and the skin surface exfoliated and hydrated. A night routine could be invaluable in keeping ageing at bay and could brilliantly delay the onset of advanced ageing.

Morning and Day Care (Steps 2 and 3) are about protecting and defending your skin from the environment you are subjecting it to. Night Care (Step 4) is about rejuvenating your skin and reversing the damage done to it during the day. In other words, if Day Care is about defence, Night Care is about attack.

1

SKIN TYPE

Dry, normal, oily, problem, sensitive or combination – how do you identify your skin type? This, the first part of Everyday, is a simple and effective way of determining your skin type so you can go out and buy or use products with ease.

2

ANTI-AGEING MORNING CARE

What does your skin need to drink the first thing in the morning? This part will cover quick,essential first-thing-in-the-morning skincare and is something you can do as easily as brushing your teeth.

3

ANTI-AGEING DAY CARE

This part will cover sunscreen buying and application. Because a big part of anti-ageing is how well you protect yourself against the sun. Part 3 will also briefly touch upon day make-up application.

4

ANTI-AGEING NIGHT CARE

Part 4 will cover night care and make-up removal and why you need a strong night routine. We will also discuss the crucial role of night repair creams and what the best age-defying ingredients are.

5

ANTI-AGEING HABITS

Sleep. Water. Supplements. Part 5 will talk about the most effective anti-ageing habits that won't just help your skin but also do wonders for the rest of your body.

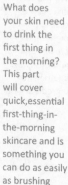

5

ANTI-AGEING HABITS

Sleep. Water. Supplements. Part 5 will talk about the most effective anti-ageing habits that won't just help your skin but also do wonders for the rest of your body.

4

ANTI-AGEING NIGHT CARE

Part 4 will cover night care and make-up removal and why you need a strong night routine. We will also discuss the crucial role of night repair creams and what the best age-defying ingredients are.

3

ANTI-AGEING DAY CARE

This part will cover sunscreen buying and application. Because a big part of anti-ageing is how well you protect yourself against the sun. Part 3 will also briefly touch upon day make-up application.

2

ANTI-AGEING MORNING CARE

What does your skin need to drink the first thing in the morning? This part will cover quick,essential first-thing-in-the-morning skincare and is something you can do as easily as brushing your teeth.

1

SKIN TYPE

Dry, normal, oily, problem, sensitive or combination – how do you identify your skin type? This, the first part of Everyday, is a simple and effective way of determining your skin type so you can go out and buy or use products with ease.

1 *What's Your Type?*

SKIN TYPE

If you've decided to shop for a brand new skincare product today, you may have a little bit of reading to do. On the pack, that is. Almost every commercially available product comes with its own suitability for your skin type and before you shop for one, understand *what* your skin type is before bringing home a bad boy. Also, do take a note of the symbol next to the skin type. We will be using that as a guide through the book.

NORMAL SKIN

Characterized by small to medium-sized pores, normal skin usually has an even and smooth texture. You'll find that very few people with normal skin suffer from acne or any other kind of skin problem.

DRY SKIN

Dry skin has small pores. Most of the time, it will feel stretched and taut. Due to the fact that this kind of skin type suffers from lack of moisture, dry skin also ages quicker, generates fine lines faster and wrinkles earlier. All of which could leave you looking older than you actually are. If you look closely, you can actually see flakes of skin on the surface.

OILY SKIN

Oily skin is classified as skin with a coarse texture containing large amounts of comedones, that is, clogged

O open pores. It has an oily sheen and can make your face look 'shiny' from time to time. Oily skin is also more prone to acne, especially during adolescence. However, if you grew up with people who had nothing better to do than to come up with nicknames for your pimples in your teens, you can have the last laugh. Oily skin ages slower than *any* other skin type. So there.

COMBINATION OR T-ZONE SKIN

T Combination skin keeps you on your toes because this is where two or more skin types converge. Your T-Zone, especially your forehead, nose and chin, could be of one skin type, possibly oily, while the rest of your face could be of another skin type, typically flaky or dry. So some parts of your face may feel dry and taut or appear dry and flaky after washing, whereas your T-zone may still feel greasy, look shiny and be prone to pimples and blackheads.

SENSITIVE SKIN

S Look but don't touch. For my clients who walk in with this type of skin, I can see thin, tiny capillaries present on the surface of the skin. As the name suggests, this skin type is acutely sensitive to many stimulants, be they sun exposure, heat and even *touch* that is, even touching the face could lead it to turn red or to break out. This kind of highly sensitive skin is often associated with hormonal imbalances and is sometimes mistaken for rosacea, another common skin problem. And it is also marked by a high degree of intolerance towards many skincare products. If you want to gift someone with this skin type something for their skin, you're better off buying them something else because this is the hardest skin type to shop for.

PROBLEM SKIN

Problem skin is a term usually used to define skin trapped in some sort of long-term chronic condition that includes severe acne, psoriasis, rosacea, seborrheic dermatitis, flaking skin or even pigmentation patches. Problem skin could be any one of the above skin types but is an additional classification indicated by the severity of the skin condition and length of treatment.

TEST FOR SKIN TYPE

1. Wash and clean your face
2. Pat dry with a towel
3. Wait for about 20 minutes
4. Stick three pieces of tape on your face:
    a. One across your forehead
    b. One down the length of your nose
    c. One across one of your cheeks by your jawline
       Note: Try not to do this in public or in front of very small children, though. You may scare people.
5. Remove the tapes after 3-5 minutes. If you see:
    a. Flakes. You have dry skin
    b. Tiny oily droplets. You have oily skin

c. A bit of both (a) and (b). You have combination skin.

d. Redness. You have sensitive skin.

6. ***What's Your Skin Type?***

> *Note it here:* _____

You're not always stuck with your skin type, though. Depending on how you age, the kinds of products you use, medical treatment, the weather you're exposed to, hormonal changes, the nutritional supplements you take and for other reasons, skin types *can* change. Skin types can sometimes also change depending on the season. If you feel that your current regimen is suddenly no longer working, you may want to take the test again to see if your skin type has altered. It could have.

5
ANTI-AGEING HABITS

Sleep. Water. Supplements. Part 5 will talk about the most effective anti-ageing habits that won't just help your skin but also do wonders for the rest of your body.

4
ANTI-AGEING NIGHT CARE

Part 4 will cover night care and make-up removal and why you need a strong night routine. We will also discuss the crucial role of night repair creams and what the best age-defying ingredients are.

3
ANTI-AGEING DAY CARE

This part will cover sunscreen buying and application. Because a big part of anti-ageing is how well you protect yourself against the sun. Part 3 will also briefly touch upon day make-up application.

2
ANTI-AGEING MORNING CARE

What does your skin need to drink the first thing in the morning? This part will cover quick,essential first-thing-in-the-morning skincare and is something you can do as easily as brushing your teeth.

1
SKIN TYPE

Dry, normal, oily, problem, sensitive or combination – how do you identify your skin type? This, the first part of Everyday, is a simple and effective way of determining your skin type so you can go out and buy or use products with ease.

Rise and Shine

ANTI-AGEING
MORNING
CARE

The problem with providing information about a morning skincare ritual is that, on the surface, it seems like every skincare expert is saying the same thing. You have to wash your face. You have to moisturize it afterwards. Simple. But when I see my clients, I realize that so many people not only ignore basic morning skincare but for many of those who actually do take the care to take care, misinformation about the right products can be quite a setback.

If I haven't emphasized it enough already, the skin is our body's largest organ and is also the most visible one. It also protects us from the onslaught of what we subject it to, to include dirt, grime, pollution and related germs and bacteria. But it's not just environmental pollution that ambushes our skin. Dead skin shedding occurs the most overnight especially while we are sleeping because that's when the skin's rejuvenating ability is at its peak. So when we wake up in the morning, even if we have washed our face before sleeping, oil has secreted from our pores, no matter what our skin type is. Cleansing the face becomes important; its function the first thing in the morning therefore is to not only remove dead skin build up but also surface oils that have accumulated overnight.

Your morning regime is a simple two-step process that should look like this:

CLEANSING

The first thing your face needs to 'drink' in the morning is water. Cleanse your face with water and a cleansing agent, which could be soap, face wash or other alternatives that I will detail in the coming pages. Avoid washing your face with hot water, though. It strips it of its moisture. As soon as you're done washing your face, pat it dry with a towel. Don't rub the towel hard all over your skin. It is abrasive and could cause breakouts.

MOISTURIZING

The second thing your skin needs to drink is moisturizer. Cleansing your face upsets the moisture balance so generously apply a moisturizer. Use as much as you need to 'cover' your face and neck. Your basic skincare is done.

Total Time
1-2 minutes

Depending on how sleepy you are, your anti-ageing morning routine shouldn't take you more than 1-2 minutes. Like I said, this is something most of you probably already know. What's less obvious, however, is deciding *what* to cleanse and moisturize with. And that is where it becomes tricky.

BUYING CLEANSERS

It's crazy. From having limited access to just a few products even 10-15 years ago, the skincare industry has just exploded. There are literally thousands of skincare products on the shelves but to make it easier, I've sifted through the good, the bad and the just plain scary to enable you to buy the best cleansing agent for your skin.

While most of my clients' problems are not due to inconsistent morning skin routines, unsuitable moisturizers or face washes have been known to make the skin look dull and rob it of its vitality. Depending on convenience and on your budget, you can either use a natural cleansing agent *or* face wash based on your skin type. Check the back of the pack for the ingredients listed in the following table.

Skin Type	Natural Cleansing Agent ₹	Face Wash Buying Guide ₹₹
N	Soak rose petals (from one large rose) in half a bottle of water overnight. In the morning, strain it, add 2 tsps of glycerine and a few drops of essential rose oil. Wet face first, apply on face, massage for thirty seconds and then wash off. This works as a good cleanser for normal skin and can be refrigerated and kept for a week.	For those with normal skin, choose a face wash with Ammonium Lauryl Ether and Ascoryl Phosphate (Vitamin C). For usage, follow instructions on the pack.

Skin Type	Natural Cleansing Agent ₹	Face Wash Buying Guide ₹₹
d	2 tbsps of curds mixed with half a grated cucumber is an effective cleanser for dry skin. Wet face first, apply on face, massage for thirty seconds and then wash off.	For dry skin, you would need to look for moisturizing agents in your face wash. Keep a lookout for Aloe Vera, Witch Hazel, Chamomile, Glycerin and Vitamin E. For usage, follow instructions on the pack.
O	Half cup of 'besan' (gram flour)mixed with half cup of raw milk works well to naturally cleanse oily skin. Wet face first, apply on face for thirty seconds and then wash off.	For oily or acne-prone skin, look out for acne-fighting elements like Salicylic Acid and Benzoyl Acid. For usage, follow instructions on the pack.
T	Half cup of curds with 1 tbsp of honey works well to cleanse combination skin. Wet face first, apply on face, massage lightly for thirty seconds and then wash off.	Look for foam-based salicylic acid face washes or Myristyl Glycol face washes as they will be not as strong as the ones used for acne-prone skin. For usage, follow instructions on the pack.

Skin Type	Natural Cleansing Agent ₹	Face Wash Buying Guide ₹₹
S	Only a trained dermatologist can tell you this.	Those with sensitive skin need face washes that are both alcohol-free and fragrance-free as these tend to be a lot gentler on delicate skin. These are usually tagged as 'hypoallergenic' face washes. However, do check with your dermatologist before making the purchase because your skin may be sensitive for other reasons, which only a trained dermatologist will be able to help you with.
D	Only a trained dermatologist can tell you this.	Only a trained dermatologist can tell you this.

ADD TO SHOPPING CART

I've designed a small 'shopping list' section that enables you to note down what you need to get as we discuss it. You can either use a natural cleansing agent or face wash to cleanse your skin, whatever suits your budget or your belief. Those with normal skin could also wash their faces with super-fatted pH soap. However, if you're using something that is already working for you, please ignore the above. But if you'd like to change your cleanser, make a note of it below:

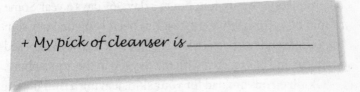

+ My pick of cleanser is _____

How should you feel afterwards?

How do you decide on what's the right cleanser for you? Well, it's a trial-and-error process. The decision between soap, face wash and natural cleanser all depends on how you feel *after* you have washed your face. The entire point of a cleanser is to feel, well, clean. And, after you rinse the cleanser off, your skin should not feel dry or parched. If you've achieved cleanliness and don't feel dry after you've washed, you've hit gold. If you're breaking out and experiencing irritation, you've not.

And are expensive cleansing options better? Natural cleansing agents are usually less expensive than soaps, which are usually less expensive than face washes. In my own practice, I've seen high-end brands killing skin texture and simple home remedies working wonders. But I've also seen premium face washes do things that no multani mitti can ever do. All that's important is whether it suits your skin and, of course, how it cleans.

BUYING MOISTURIZERS

So why moisturize? Well, it is connected with the oil secretion on your face. Your face secretes oil all the time. Many reasons, including genetics, seasonal changes, usage of incorrect products, hormonal defects and stress, could trigger excess oil production twenty-four hours a day, 365 days a year. Some of that oil is fresh while the rest has been lying on your skin for a while and has been oxidized, that is, it has been exposed to the air and has reacted with the oxygen in the atmosphere.

Oxidized oils are bad for your skin, leaving a thin film of unwanted germs and bacteria, which could clog your pores while fresh skin oil, on the other hand, is the best natural moisturizing agent. We need to wash off the bad oils. What would be amazing – and, quite frankly, magical – is if your cleanser could wash off the oxidized oil and keep the fresh skin oil. But fresh and oxidized oils mix with each other and you can't separate the two. They are stuck together, joined at the hip like Siamese twins, leaving you with no choice but to wash off *all* oils and replenish the lost fresh oil through the process of moisturization.

Secondly, it is important to remember that the skin's natural ability to moisturize diminishes as we get older; the skin produces less oil with age. This impacts the skin's natural ability to stay hydrated. In other words, the need for a moisturizer will only increase, not decrease, as you grow older.[1] Do try and remember that the drier your skin,

[1] Neil Sadick with Samantha Marshall and Adam Dinkes, *The New Natural: Your Ultimate Guide to Scalpel-Free Age Reversal* (New York: Rodale, 2011).

1. The darker it gets
2. The faster it ages
3. The itchier it gets

A good moisturizer will:
1. Seal in the moisture
2. Smooth and repair the skin
3. Attract moisture to the skin

HUMECTANTS

The job of a humectant is to attract moisture to your skin both from the deeper layers of the skin as well as from the atmosphere. Panthenol, urea, lactic acid and glycerin are common humectants.

EMOLLIENTS

Emollients repair and smoothen the skin and include oils and lipids like stearic acid, mineral oil and lanolin. The creamier the moisturizer, the more emollient it is.

OCCLUSIVES

The work of sealing in the moisture is done by occlusives like petroleum jelly and paraffin. These prevent moisture from escaping by creating a 'sealing-in' layer on your skin.

In other words, a good moisturizer is therefore an effective blend of humectants, emollients and occlusives. In the moisturizing guide below, you can either use a natural moisturizer *or* a commercial moisturizer to nourish your skin. However, just like with cleansers, if you're using something that is already working for you, you can ignore the options below:

Skin Type	Natural/Economical Moisturizers' Guide ₹	Commercial/Premium Moisturizers' Buying Guide ₹₹
n	Homemade mayonnaise is a great moisturizer for normal skin. Dab it on your face, slather for sixty seconds, wait for 2-3 minutes and then wash off.	Look for moisturizers with glycerin or petroleum (found in Vaseline). For usage, follow instructions on the pack.
d	Take 2 tbsps of either coconut oil, almond oil or olive oil, add one egg and 1 tsp of lime juice to it. Mix well and leave it on the skin for ten minutes. Wash and pat dry.	Medicated lotion with urea and lactic acid works well to moisturize dry skin. For usage, follow instructions on the pack.
o	Honey can be used to moisturize oily skin. Dab it on your face, slather for sixty seconds, wait for 2-3 minutes and then wash off.	It's a myth that people with oily skin don't need to moisturize. If you have oily skin, choose a moisturizer that is lightweight, non-comedogenic (won't clog your pores) and oil-free. For usage, follow instructions on the pack.

Skin Type	Natural/Economical Moisturizers' Guide ₹	Commercial/Premium Moisturizers' Buying Guide ₹₹
T	Crushed overripe fruit pulp can be used as a moisturizer for combination skin. Dab it on your face, slather for sixty seconds, wait for 2-3 minutes and then wash off.	Water-based moisturisers are the best for combination skin as they are light and non-greasy. Look for ones with dimethicone or hyaluronic acid. For usage, follow instructions on the pack.
S	Only a trained dermatologist can tell you this.	If you have sensitive skin or a skin condition, moisturizing regularly can help reduce some of the irritation. Please check with your dermatologist for options.
D	Only a trained dermatologist can tell you this.	Only a trained dermatologist can tell you this.

How should your skin feel afterwards?

A good moisturizer should make you feel hydrated and fresh. It should not make your skin feel 'suffocated' and 'trapped'. Having a long-term relationship with the right moisturizer is a trial-and-error process and sometimes the simplest solutions work best.

Always cleanse before you moisturize. In my experience, moisturizers work best if you remove dead skin cells first before adding the cream or lotion and that is something that will be done by your cleanser or face wash; cleansers mildly exfoliate your skin. This will help your skin absorb the moisturizer better and will also improve hydration. For best results, moisturize *moist* skin. Apply the moisturizer within *three* minutes of washing your face. This traps the moisture already present on the skin.

Please note that a winter moisturizer won't work in the summer; it'll be too heavy and may clog your pores. Moisturizers have to be changed according to season. Additionally, in some climates and situations, you may need to moisturize more often.

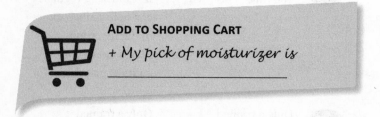

ADD TO SHOPPING CART

+ *My pick of moisturizer is*

_____

DO YOU HAVE TEN MORE MINUTES?
EVERYDAY BODY CARE
Bathing

We're a hot, dusty, tropical country. Heat and dust mean sweat and grime. And grime means bathing. I'd recommend bathing twice daily, if possible. I'd also say that whether you use soap, shower gel, loofahs, pumice stone or anything else, so long as you feel clean, refreshed and your skin doesn't feel parched or over-dry after bathing (that parched feeling is due to the fact that the pH of your skin has changed due to the detergents present in the soap), then what you use to cleanse your body doesn't matter. Because the skin on your body is not as delicate as the skin on your face.

So long as you feel hydrated and your skin feels good, what you use to moisturize your body doesn't matter either. To moisturize your body, you can quickly rub oil (preferably coconut oil with a few drops of eucalyptus if you want to neutralize the coconut aroma) all over your body immediately before bathing. Don't wash it all off. Let some remain. This thin film of oil protects the body from the escape of water from the skin (which is also called TEWL or Trans-epidermal Water Loss). Alternatively, use any good commercially available body lotion that softens your skin, unless you have an existing skin condition, which needs medical assistance in which case it's better to use moisturizers that contain urea and lactic acid which penetrate deeper. Ask your doctor first though, if your condition is severe.

Lips

1. Chapped lips can be treated with any good lip balm or Vaseline. Or even ghee. Yes, ghee. It locks in moisture and is great for healing dry lips.

2. Whether you're faced with the most nerve-wracking interview, the yummiest dessert, the hottest Bollywood heartthrob or the world's sexiest shoes, try not to lick your lips. Even if you are only just trying to moisten them, licking the lips ironically causes them to further dry out.

3. While we're still on the lips, remember to use your toothbrush gently – *very* gently – to exfoliate dead skin cells from the lips *after* you have finished brushing your teeth while the bristles are still soft.

Feet

1. Dry heels can be treated with creams containing salicylic acid. You can do this at night. Just before you sleep, wash your feet, apply the cream, wrap each foot in a shower cap followed by covering each foot with a loose cotton sock. Heel yourself.

2. For cracked heels, a medically prescribed exfoliating salicylic acid cream with keratolytic agent softens and moisturizes the skin as well as helps exfoliate dead skin cells. Mix this cream with a little Vaseline, or something similar, apply on the feet at night and cover with a cling film to ensure the cream remains in contact with the skin. Cracked heels will heal beautifully over time and your feet will feel smooth and soft.

The above will in total add about ten minutes to your daily routine (even lesser if you don't have dry feet or lips). The question is: **Do You Have Ten More Minutes?**

DEEPLY DIPPY
DEEP MOISTURIZATION

1. For deep moisturization, opt for moisturizing and hydrating face treatments like ionization, which enable hydrating creams to penetrate the deeper layers of the skin by using a mild electric current.

2. A full-body oil massage helps you to de-stress, hydrates your body, gives the entire body a glow and prevents skin dryness, which in turn delays ageing.

WATCH YOUR TONE
WHEN TONER IS RECOMMENDED

Toners were recommended earlier for two reasons. One, to maintain the pH balance of the skin after cleansing because the soap or cleanser may have interfered with it and second,to remove stale make-up or for deep-pore cleaning.

While toners are still extremely popular with celebs, actors and those working in the world of glamour, unless your skin is very oily or the make-up is very difficult to remove, toners aren't really necessary. If you must, get a toner that helps to smoothen, soften and repair the skin. Just ensure that it's not alcohol-based, as it'll dry the skin. A toner is a nice addition to your skincare routine. But it's only that. An addition.

1

SKIN TYPE

Dry, normal, oily, problem, sensitive or combination – how do you identify your skin type? This, the first part of Everyday, is a simple and effective way of determining your skin type so you can go out and buy or use products with ease.

2

ANTI-AGEING MORNING CARE

What does your skin need to drink the first thing in the morning? This part will cover quick, essential first-thing-in-the-morning skincare and is something you can do as easily as brushing your teeth.

3

ANTI-AGEING DAY CARE

This part will cover sunscreen buying and application. Because a big part of anti-ageing is how well you protect yourself against the sun. Part 3 will also briefly touch upon day make-up application.

4

ANTI-AGEING NIGHT CARE

Part 4 will cover night care and make-up removal and why you need a strong night routine. We will also discuss the crucial role of night repair creams and what the best age-defying ingredients are.

5

ANTI-AGEING HABITS

Sleep. Water. Supplements. Part 5 will talk about the most effective anti-ageing habits that won't just help your skin but also do wonders for the rest of your body.

3

ANTI-AGEING
DAY CARE

May Day

In a hot, tropical country like ours, it is unbelievable how many people take sun care for granted. My clients seem to be okay with allowing themselves to be poked, prodded and injected without putting in place one of the simplest, most fundamental and preventive anti-ageing processes that would take them less than a few minutes a day to institute. Sunscreen.

I think the problem is that growing up in a hot, sunny climate and never really fussing about the sun as children (even though children need sunscreen as well) leads to the idea that it's not worth fussing about as adults. We think it's inconsequential, just one of those things that we've grown up with.

I cannot emphasize enough that the sun is one of the biggest ageing threats in the environment. And you don't have to be out of the house or under shelter for it to not impact you. If you're sitting next to a sunny window reading this book, it's ageing you. If the sun's rays are reaching you or are in your vicinity, they are ageing you. You could even be sitting at home, but if its rays are reaching you, it's still ageing you.

Of course, you want to be outside under the sun getting on with your life. This two-step process for anti-ageing day care includes both sunscreen as well as make-up selection and application so you can start your day, play and make hay. While the sun shines.

SUNSCREEN

Cover all parts of your face and neck with sunscreen about twenty minutes before you get out and even if you are at home. Reapply every 2-4 hours or as per the instructions on the pack. Sorry, let me say that again. *Drown* all parts of your face and neck in sunscreen. It is one of the few parts of my 'Less Is More' skincare philosophy where 'More Is Less'. And sunscreen is crucial for both children and adults.

MAKE-UP

This is a make-up selection and application guide for those of you who use make-up at the beginning of your day. As this is not an anti-ageing part of your day care routine, it's not included in the total time taken for your daily anti-ageing care.

Total Time

1 minute

SUN DAMAGE

Sunlight consists of multiple ultraviolet rays, which are part of the sun's (electromagnetic) light spectrum:[2] Ultraviolet A (UVA), Ultraviolet B (UVB) and Ultraviolet C (UVC) and infrared rays. While research on what damage these rays do gets updated all the time, we do know that UVA ages us and UVB burns us. UVC rays, while being the strongest, are too short to reach us;it is mostly absorbed by the ozone layer of the earth, and is the least of our sun-related problems.

[2] 'Understanding UVA and UVB', accessed 30 December 2014, http://www.skincancer.org/prevention/uva-and-uvb/understanding-uva-and-uvb.

KNOW YOUR RAYS

UVA Rays

1. Are more widely prevalent than UVB rays, and are present rain or shine, at all hours of the day.
2. Account for about 95 per cent of the total UV radiation we are exposed to.[3]
3. Can pass through glass. 70 per cent of the rays penetrate clear/plain glass while 30-50 per cent can pass through tinted/reflective glass.
4. Can cause wrinkles, sun tan, allergies, fine lines, photoageing, blemishes.
5. Are present throughout the year.
6. Penetrate all the way deep below the epidermis and reach the dermis, which is the layer that has nerves, blood vessels, connective tissues, hair follicles and glands, causing damage to include deep wrinkles, excessive pigmentation and a weakened or compromised immune system, which can show itself up years later.[4]
7. Are carcinogenic.[5] This is especially true for Caucasian skin.

UVB Rays

1. Are more intense at higher altitudes, in the summer months and between 10 a.m. to 4 p.m., especially on sunny days.

[3] Ibid.
[4] Neil Sadick, *The New Natural.*
[5] 'Understanding UVA and UVB', accessed 30 December 2014.

2. Can't pass through glass.
3. Cause burns, not wrinkles.
4. Help the body make Vitamin D.
5. Are also carcinogenic. Have the potential to cause skin cancer, especially in Caucasian skin.

As a separate note, infra-red rays can also cause premature ageing and pigmentation problems.

BUYING SUNSCREEN

The key objective of sunscreen is to protect yourself from *both* UVA and UVB radiations. But not all sunscreens are created equal. They come with different formulations with varying degrees of protection. So then, what is enough? Given below, in a nutshell, is what your sunscreen *must* have when you are buying it:

Your Chosen Sunscreen	
A. *Sun Protection Factor (SPF)*	*Above 30*
B. *PA Protection (PA +++)*	
C. *Sunscreen Compounds*	
Zinc Oxide	
Titanium Dioxide	
Benzophenone, Mexoryl and Octicrylene	

Your sunscreen *must* have the following:

1. **SPF**

   Sun Protection Factor. This should be at a minimum of 30. The higher the SPF, the better protection it offers

you from the UVB rays of the sun. How it works is that
if the SPF is 15, for example, and you're out in the sun
for ten minutes, you are protected fifteen times. Doing
the math, ten minutes of sun exposure means that you
are protected for (10 x 15) 150 minutes or two-and-a-
half hours. Which is why reapplication of sunscreen is
so important as your day progresses.

2. **PA Protection**

As SPF only offers you protection from UVB rays,
your sunscreen also needs to protect you from UVA
rays. For this, it's important that the product also has
PA protection. Look out for the PA+++ sign when you
buy sunscreen.

3. **Sunscreen Compounds**

Your sunscreen should contain the following
compounds as well:

a. Zinc oxide and titanium dioxide, which act as
   sunblocks preventing the sun's rays from penetrating
   deep into your skin

b. Compounds like benophenone, mexoryl and
   octicrylene, which also protect against UVA rays.

Your sunscreen should therefore have an SPF of 30 and
above, have a PA +++ protection and have the above
compounds listed on the pack.

Additional sunscreen wish list:

4. **Photostability**

Your chosen sunscreen should also be photostable,
that is, storing it for weeks at a time should not affect
its efficacy.

5. **Compatibility**

   It shouldn't irritate your skin. There are sunscreens designed for users who have the tendency to develop acne or clogged pores.

USING SUNSCREEN

1. Apply an *extremely* thick coat of sunscreen about twenty minutes before you step out. Optimum quantity is about 3 ml (a little more than ½ tsp) for the face and neck, and an additional 1 tsp for the arms and 2 tsps for the legs. Use on all exposed parts of your body. This is the only place where I believe that *More Is Less*. You can never get too much of sunscreen.

2. Depending on the SPF (at a minimum of 30), reapply it every 2-4 hours. Repetition is the *only* sure-fire way to make it effective. And as we now know, since UVA rays can penetrate both clear and tinted glass, even if you are indoors or are travelling in a car, sunscreen must be applied. If you're on a beach or mountainous holiday, SPF of 50 is better. Further, new research suggests that while SPF is important, it is not as important as the repeated use of sunscreen at regular intervals.

3. Make your sunscreen compatible with your skin. Mattifying or gel-based sunscreens work for oily skin, sunscreens with moisturizing factors suit dry skin and any regular OTC (Over The Counter) sunscreens work well for normal skin.

4. Try to avoid sun exposure between 10 a.m. to 4 p.m. if possible.

5. Realize that you are exposed to UV radiation and

infra-red rays in both hot *and* cold climes. If the sun is reaching you no matter what the outside temperature, you will *still* burn or age from exposure. Don't forget to exercise extra caution near water, snowy or sandy places as these destinations intensify sun coverage.

6. Use a lip balm with an SPF of 15 at the very least.

7. You can use a waterproof sunscreen when you're swimming. But you would need to reapply it every forty minutes as the effect wears off faster when you're in water.

8. *Sunscreens will not prevent your skin from tanning*; they will just protect you from the effects of harmful UV radiation.

9. Do also note that the same sunscreen could react differently in different weather conditions: the same product that was perfect in the winter could make you feel sticky during the monsoon.

10. Always keep sunscreen handy and take it with you in your bag.

11. Additionally, try and physically protect yourself from the sun with the help of scarves, hats, long sleeves, sunglasses or even covering your face with a dupatta. It helps significantly but you still need to wear sunscreen or sunblock.

12. Sun protection should start as early as the age of six months to a year.

13. I feel that many of my clients are reluctant to use sunscreen as they find it too greasy or feel it makes the skin take on an unnatural film of white. High-tech sunscreens now have micronized tiny particles that

leave no film on the face. Additionally, some of the newer sunscreens can be applied even five minutes before leaving the house. Please read the label carefully.

14. If your sunscreen comes with moisturizers or if you have an SPF in your moisturizer, use it separately anyway. The more layers you have, the better protected you are.

15. Lastly, there are *no* natural or effective homemade alternatives to sunscreen so get a good commercial sunscreen after doing a little browsing. It is something you will never regret.

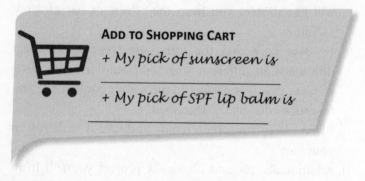

ADD TO SHOPPING CART

+ *My pick of sunscreen is*

_____

+ *My pick of SPF lip balm is*

_____

HERE COMES THE SUN

It's always good to get a D on your health report card. Vitamin D, that is. But the deficiency of this vitamin has become alarmingly common. And it's not specific to life stage: my ninety-three-year-old mother, my eighty-four-year-old father, my thirty-year-old son (who plays a lot of outdoor sports) and I *all* tested positive for Vitamin D deficiency.

While I have elaborated on how sun exposure ages you, unfortunately too little exposure to the sun doesn't help your cause either. Our bodies do not naturally create Vitamin D and the rays of the sun help us synthesize it. We use Vitamin D to balance the levels of calcium and phosphorus in our blood and bones. We also use it to enable the storage of calcium in our bones. Further, exposure to the sun may also help destroy germs and bacteria.

Sunbathing for Vitamin D is best done very early in the morning at sunrise when the sun's heat is not as strong, or as ageing. Better yet, just take an early morning walk and get some exercise out of it. Recommended sun exposure is a minimum of five minutes to a maximum of thirty per day.

Photoageing: Above is an example of how the sun damages the face. The left half of the face has photoaged.

MAKE-UP SELECTION AND APPLICATION

While this is not really anti-ageing, here are a few things I've learnt about applying make-up for the day:

1. In general, ensure that your skin type is well suited to the kind of products you use. While on the face of it, this seems fairly obvious, it is a surprisingly

common mistake many women make. Try and use the 'acclimatize' approach when buying and trying on new make-up. As opposed to investing straight off the bat in a big bottle of expensive foundation, for example, using a free tester at the make-up outlet, test it on the back of your neck or behind the ears. See if your skin reacts; if it doesn't, only then should you go ahead.

2. Less is always more for day make-up. Try to avoid heavy foundations during the day unless absolutely necessary. As many of you may already know, make-up oxidizes on coming in contact with the oxygen in the air. Heavy, oxidized make-up combined with sweat, grime and the day's pollution is a cocktail of bacteria sitting on your skin. Light concealers, however, used to touch up smaller parts of the face, are not so overwhelming for the day and can be used with beautiful effect.

3. After your morning routine, in order of hierarchy, make-up should be the *last* thing you put on before you leave for the day, right after your sunscreen. You can apply the second coat of sunscreen over your face – and therefore over your make-up – in the middle of the day. You can touch up your make-up after this, if you like.

TO BB OR NOT TO BB

What's hot on the make-up horizon right now is the BB cream or the Blemish Balm. BB creams were originally formulated by dermatologists for patients recovering from laser skin surgeries. They are unique in that not only do they provide coverage in the form of a foundation or primer, they also are essentially tinted moisturizers with broad spectrum SPF and antioxidants.

BB creams definitely work for people who are on the go and want to use one cream instead of two or three because the same formulation has a soothing agent, a moisturizing agent, a covering agent (the foundation or primer), a protection agent (SPF), anti-ageing agents (antioxidants) *and* it's easy to use. Having said that, though, I would still add sunscreen and moisturizer and would look at a BB as extra protection and benefit. Because you can never have enough protection from the sun.

DOES THE SKIN NEED TO BREATHE?

That's a myth. Make-up and dirt clog your pores, not night creams and moisturizers, with the exception of a few heavy products that can clog pores.

5

ANTI-AGEING HABITS

Sleep. Water. Supplements. Part 5 will talk about the most effective anti-ageing habits that won't just help your skin but also do wonders for the rest of your body.

4

ANTI-AGEING NIGHT CARE

Part 4 will cover night care and make-up removal and why you need a strong night routine. We will also discuss the crucial role of night repair creams and what the best age-defying ingredients are.

3

ANTI-AGEING DAY CARE

This part will cover sunscreen buying and application. Because a big part of anti-ageing is how well you protect yourself against the sun. Part 3 will also briefly touch upon day make-up application.

2

ANTI-AGEING MORNING CARE

What does your skin need to drink the first thing in the morning? This part will cover quick, essential first-thing-in-the-morning skincare and is something you can do as easily as brushing your teeth.

1

SKIN TYPE

Dry, normal, oily, problem, sensitive or combination – how do you identify your skin type? This, the first part of Everyday, is a simple and effective way of determining your skin type so you can go out and buy or use products with ease.

While You Were Sleeping

ANTI-AGEING NIGHT CARE

When you turn off that night light, scrunch up your pillow and start the process of ending your day with a good night's sleep, you've gone to bed but your body hasn't. This is when rejuvenation is at its peak as cell turnover increases at night. Ingredients in anti-ageing night creams capitalize on this biological process. *That's* the best time to use anti-ageing creams. While you are sleeping.

MAKE-UP REMOVAL

For those of you who use make-up, this is a short guide on how you should remove make-up.

CLEANSING

Wash off the grime and oil at night. Follow the same cleansing routine as you do in the morning.

ANTI-AGEING NIGHT CREAM

The last thing you need to do before sleeping is repairing and rejuvenating your skin. Here, we will also talk about what best suits your skin.

Total Time 5 minutes

Even if you aren't looking for an anti-ageing solution, night care is still one of the easiest and best things you can do for your skin. And all this just adds five minutes to your nightly teeth-brushing routine.

MAKE-UP REMOVAL

Subjecting your skin to layers of foundation, kajal, blush and other stuff is one thing. Being casual about your make-up removal is another thing altogether. Stale make-up can clog your pores,make your skin oily and cause break outs.

For the eyes, it's better to use a separate, oil-based eye make-up remover as eye make-up is more intricately embedded and, therefore, more stubborn. This is how I remove eye make-up: I soak a cotton pad in eye-make-up remover, close my eyes and place it over one eye. I hold it for five seconds, then wipe in a downward motion from the lids to the lashes. I then flip the cotton pad over to the clean side, and carefully and gently wipe the upper and lower eyelid margin. Alternatively, you can use an ear bud dipped in remover to remove eyelid make-up.

For the face, use baby oil with cotton if you don't have oily, problem or sensitive skin. Else, a face make-up remover works equally well. Toners are best for deep, stubborn make-up. For eye and face make-up removal, you could also use high-quality make-up removal tissues.

I've had clients who eventually identified the cause of their frequent breakouts as make-up removers, so shop with care. Like I have said before, if you have a good make-up removal system, ignore the shopping list below; else do your research and see what works for you:

ADD TO SHOPPING CART

+ My pick of eye make-up remover is _____

+ My pick of face make-up remover is

CLEANSING

Make-up removal could still leave trace residue from the product and, in some cases, stale make-up. So cleanse your face because mere make-up removal is not enough. When it comes to cleansing, what you do in the morning, you should do at night.

NIGHT CREAM

When a client walking in for a first-time consultation sets down a bag full of creams on my table with a slightly bewildered expression, I know that they have been bombarded by too many choices and, when in doubt, have bought it all. Night creams are a bit like multivitamins. A company may market Brand X multivitamin as an 'energy booster' while another company may position their multivitamin as a 'revitalizer', but if you flip the pack over and read the compositions, many – or all – ingredients will overlap in some form or the other. I always solve this problem by telling them that if they have bought too many brands, they can use one after the other, one at a time.

Start night repair as early as possible because the younger you start, the longer you delay the onset of ageing. While the difference between the cell turnover rate in your teens to the time you are in your fifties is large, there are still ways you can speed up the turnover rate as you age. And it's never too late to start the process of night repair even if you're over sixty and reading this.

WHEN SHOULD YOU START NIGHT CREAMS?

While anti-ageing night creams are usually recommended for those above thirty-five, twenty-five is the new thirty-five.

You can start either *when* or *before* you see the following signs:

1. First signs of fine lines
2. Dryness of the skin
3. Mild pigmentation patches
4. Sun damage/photoageing

You can also start if you knowingly follow an ageing lifestyle and are looking for something to repair the inevitable damage.

BUYING GUIDE

Your night repair companion must have the first three ingredients of the following. The rest depend on your skin condition.

1. **Retinol**: The most active and purest form of Vitamin A. Great for skin cell turnover. Next to sunscreen, retinol is one of the most crucial anti-ageing elements you can have in your arsenal.
2. **Retinyl Palmitate**: It is derived from Retinol and is a form of Vitamin A. It is often referred to as the 'skin

vitamin'. It is best known for its anti-wrinkle effect on the skin and is one of the most popular ingredients for skincare as well as cosmetic products.

3. **Peptides:** Encourages cell turnover. Peptides also work beautifully towards increasing collagen production during the night.

4. **Phytic Acid:** It is derived from plants, and is a natural plant antioxidant. It blocks the formation of excess melanin and is best known for its skin brightening abilities.

5. **Ascorbic Acid:** It is a topical Vitamin C. Helps repair damaged skin and protects it from further damage.

6. **Allantoin:** Promotes healing. Has soothing, moisturizing and skin softening qualities, thereby promoting skin renewal.

7. **Kojic Acid:** Great for pigmentation problems. Kojic Acid inhibits melanin production.

8. **Alpha-arbutin:** Great for brightening the skin because it blocks epidermal melanin production. It is also great for reducing skin tanning after sun exposure.

9. **Glycerine:** Attracts water to the skin. Keeps it hydrated.

10. **Glycerlystearate:** It is a wax-like chemical product, forming a barrier on the skin. It controls the loss of moisture thus providing protection from free radicals.

11. **Azelaic Acid:** Works for acne, skin discolourations and skin rejuvenation.

It is vital that your night cream has Retinol, Retinyl Palmitate and the trendy new kid on the block, Peptides. The rest of the ingredients can depend on your existing skin condition and the problem area you want to target. For example, if you want to sort out your pigmentation problems, maybe you could choose a night cream with Kojic Acid. So your chosen brand will now have Retinol, Retinyl Palmitate, Peptides and Kojic Acid in it. Do your research, shop around a bit and see what works for you:

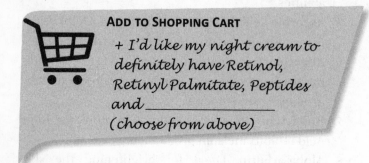

ADD TO SHOPPING CART

+ *I'd like my night cream to definitely have Retinol, Retinyl Palmitate, Peptides and _____ (choose from above)*

USAGE OF CREAMS

When I sent one of my clients off with prescriptions and solutions for her dull and acne-prone skin, I was expecting to see a visibly brighter, smoother face at her follow-up appointment. It was exactly the opposite. Her skin was redder, had blotches and looked angry. Like she did. A cursory check revealed that she had misunderstood the amount she had to use. Instead of using a 'dot' of the product as instructed, she was using a toothpaste-sized helping. It was an honest mistake but to prevent you from repeating it, I've come up with a system which I hope can prevent topical cream's biggest folly: over medication.

Topical creams are:

- Best used under medical supervision
- Less is always more
- Can cause skin irritation when used in excess
- Is to be avoided before and after skin treatments like peels, lasers, bleaching, cleanups and facials, unless specified by your doctor.

GOING DOTTY: DR PAI'S DOT SYSTEM

If you're seeing spots in front of your eyes, then I've done my job. My Dot System is for all kinds of prescription creams that you may need to use in conjunction with your night cream. Ointments, serums or whatever else your doctor prescribes should preferably be precisely administered in these kanjoos, stingy quantities. You want to exploit the cream's potency. You don't want your skin to be damaged by it.

- **The Pinhead Dot**: The first dot on the left is the dosage I prescribe for creams with Retinol or for Retinoic creams.
- **The Chana Dal Dot**: The dot second from the left should be about the size of a grain of chana dal. This is my recommended dosage for anti-acne night creams and anti-acne formulations.
- **The Small Green Pea Dot**: The third dot from the left is best for serums.

- **The Kabuli Chana/Chick Pea Dot**: The dot on the extreme right is the prescribed dosage for body areas.

The best way to administer the above 'dot' dosages is to first dab the cream on the fingers and only then spread it on the face. In order of sequence, prescription topical creams should be applied first and only then should they be followed by a generous helping of your night cream.

Night care done well will reflect changes in 2-3 weeks. No matter where you are on the ageing continuum, your skin will feel more taut, you'll see fewer lines and lesser pigmentation; overall, your skin will be smoother and well moisturized.

And all this while you were sleeping.

HOME SAFE

Listed below are daily cures and homemade solutions for common skin problems. This is in addition to your daily skin routine. However, you can check these with a doctor or a trusted cosmetologist before using.

For	Do It Yourself
Acne	Apply fresh mint juice to your face every night for a few minutes to cure pimples without drying out your skin. Mint is full of beneficial minerals and vitamins.
Dull Skin	Tomato is amazing for the skin as it is not only rich in Vitamin C and Vitamin A but eliminates excess oils and also possesses astringent properties, which contribute significantly in brightening dull skin.

For	*Do It Yourself*

To avail of these benefits, what you need to do is apply the pulp of a tomato on your face – including the area under the eye – and leave it on for about twenty minutes. Wash it off with warm water. Repeat daily for a good complexion.

Or, mix one teaspoon of gram flour or besan, a pinch of turmeric powder, a few drops of lime juice and half a teaspoon of milk, and add water to get a smooth paste. Apply this all over your face – including the area under the eye – and leave on for thirty minutes. Wash off with water.

The lactic acid in the milk as well as the lime juice mildly exfoliate and brighten the skin. Turmeric, being a fantastic antiseptic, helps with any acne, if needed. Besan is the exfoliating agent and the base of this scrub.

Normal/ Dry Skin Maintenance

For those with normal or dry skin, delay wrinkles and offset dryness with this cabbage mask. Grind a few cabbage leaves and extract their juice. To this cabbage juice, add a teaspoon of honey and a quarter of a teaspoon of yeast. Mix this well and apply a thick coat over your face and neck. Leave it on for fifteen minutes before washing it off. The cabbage in the mask is a superb source of Vitamin C and is extremely good at repairing wear and tear.

For	Do It Yourself
Oily Skin Maintenance	The classics are always the best. A pack of multani mitti (Fuller's earth) and rose water heals and dries acne-prone skin.
Mature Skin	To firm up mature skin – that is, of people over the age of fifty or skin that has aged quickly – a paste made of a teaspoon of olive oil and an egg white really works when it is applied on the face and neck, allowed to dry for twenty minutes, then washed off with cold water.

5
ANTI-AGEING HABITS

Sleep. Water. Supplements. Part 5 will talk about the most effective anti-ageing habits that won't just help your skin but also do wonders for the rest of your body.

4
ANTI-AGEING NIGHT CARE

Part 4 will cover night care and make-up removal and why you need a strong night routine. We will also discuss the crucial role of night repair creams and what the best age-defying ingredients are.

3
ANTI-AGEING DAY CARE

This part will cover sunscreen buying and application. Because a big part of anti-ageing is how well you protect yourself against the sun. Part 3 will also briefly touch upon day make-up application.

2
ANTI-AGEING MORNING CARE

What does your skin need to drink the first thing in the morning? This part will cover quick, essential first-thing-in-the-morning skincare and is something you can do as easily as brushing your teeth.

1
SKIN TYPE

Dry, normal, oily, problem, sensitive or combination – how do you identify your skin type? This, the first part of Everyday, is a simple and effective way of determining your skin type so you can go out and buy or use products with ease.

ANTI-AGEING HABITS

Anti-Ageing on the Inside

Delaying ageing is a complete solution that has to emerge from *within* your body. Like with what you eat, and whether you exercise (both of which we will talk about later in this book), this, the last part of Everyday, outlines daily habits that age us and what we can do to turn things around.

SLEEP

Sleep aids cell turnover and regeneration like little else can. This part focuses on how sleep impacts your skin.

SUPPLEMENTS

Vitamin A or C? B1 or B2? What's the best for your skin and how to avoid the common mistake of overmedication.

WATER

Slurp. Drink up for better skin.

WHAT SLEEP DOES TO YOUR SKIN

Everyone and their aunt can tell when you've had a rough night and haven't logged in your sleeping hours. The skin sags a bit, under-eye bags seem to be more prominent or the skin seems to have lost a bit of its lustre. Your skin could also look dehydrated, the eyes puffy or the complexion sallow or even ashy. Sleep deprivation causes blood vessels to dilate resulting in dark circles (that is, if you are not already genetically predisposed to forming dark circles). You need to sleep to save your skin.

But we all know this. The importance of a good night's sleep for the skin and for the rest of the body has been researched, documented and endorsed by skincare experts, doctors and celebs. But yet, in the crazy circus of our lives, we often forget to follow through with this one final step.

Sleeping is the time when our bodies repair and renew themselves. The nervous system has two states: the sympathetic system that is more in control when we are awake and the parasympathetic system that takes over when we are sleeping. The sympathetic system keeps the blood flow closer to the core of the body while the parasympathetic system ensures that the blood flow shifts outwards to our skin. In other words, when we sleep, our skin benefits from the heightened blood flow and the oxygen the blood brings with it. That's when the skin gets a chance to best repair itself. But when you don't sleep or don't sleep enough, you're not giving the skin a chance to heal. In addition, at night, the skin is not exposed to pollutants and the sun, giving it a greater chance to get back on the mend.

Sleep is a stress reliever, reducing the presence of cortisol, which is the stress hormone and which is also responsible for thinning skin, stretch marks and discolouration. Sleep also increases melatonin, the sleep hormone, which fights age spots, fine lines and even skin cancer. Your nightly shut-eye can also make special growth hormones more efficient, leading to the repair and regeneration of collagen-producing cells, which are attributed to skin elasticity and tightness.

But, like with everything else in life, it is not just quantity, it is quality. How long is just as important as how *well*. While even superficial sleep helps skin cells repair and rebuild, most of the skin's cell turnover and regeneration work takes place during deep sleep, also called REM [rapid eye movement] sleep. Deep sleep is needed for deep repair.

I can give you tips on how to sleep better. I can tell you to avoid caffeine, heavy meals, sugary food and any other stimulant a few hours before sleeping. I can tell you to ensure that the ambience of the bedroom is soothing, clutter-free and that you should kick your TV out. I can also tell you to clear your mind, finish your important tasks, keep no pending issues that may disturb your sleep or will keep you up at night. But I feel that it's something that will only be done once you consider sleep crucial for your well-being. Not just for your skin but for the overall quality of the rest of your life.

WHAT SUPPLEMENTS DO FOR YOUR SKIN

Besides the medications, creams, jars, bottles and general care, nutritional supplements are an imperative tool for the anti-ageing process and have the added benefit of treating many other health problems. Anti-ageing and other deficiencies share almost the same set of supplements – also called neutraceuticals – that include vitamins, antioxidants, calcium, iron and fish oil capsules.

However, it's important to take supplements at a time in our lives when we need them. I believe that, on an average, till about the age of forty, supplements aren't necessary unless otherwise prescribed by your practitioner in cases of disease, deficiencies, metabolic disorders or even if you are undergoing weight training. Supplements are also a fairly crucial part of some of the most important life stages of a woman including pregnancy, lactation, perimenopause and menopause. Lack of calcium could intensify, or lead to, osteoporosis; lack of B12 can cause depression, fatigue and tremours; fish oil supplements can control cholesterol; and Co-enzyme Q10 is a cardiac energizer.

As with any other medical information in this book, it is best to not self-medicate but check with your doctor if you can take these. And if you are already taking multivitamins, it is also important to know exactly what it contains so you don't take, say, a Vitamin C and a multivitamin with Vitamin C at the same time. Overdosage can lead to toxicity. Remember, despite their colourful, innocent look, vitamins and supplements are *not* harmless if they are abused.

WHAT WATER DOES FOR YOUR SKIN

All the organs of the body need water. And the cells of the skin, just like all the other organs, are made up primarily of water. When skin cells don't get enough water, the skin turns dry, flaky and tight. Dry skin is wrinkle-prone and not as resilient as hydrated skin.

On an everyday basis, we lose a great deal of water via perspiration, bowel movement and more. Even when we breathe, we lose water through the process of condensation. Drinking up is the only way to replace the loss. And now, for the bad news: the skin is the *last* organ to receive the water we drink. And that's why we moisturize: to hydrate it from the outside.

How much water is enough?

- Two to two-and-a-half litres is enough; that is your magic number. That's 8-10 (250 ml) glasses of water a day.

- Three litres, that is, twelve glasses of water, is required only if you sweat too much either because of the climate you live in, your profession (medical representatives or door-to-door salespeople) or if you play sports.
- Four litres is in excess and I don't recommend it unless you're on some sort of short-term detox diet.
- This is pure water consumption I'm talking about though. Consumption of tea, coffee, juice, aerated beverages and so on are not included here. The intake of water itself should be about 8-10 glasses every day.

While the benefits to your skin may not be immediately felt, investing just a few weeks in increasing your water intake should start showing good results.

WHAT SMOKING AND DRINKING DO *NOT* DO FOR YOUR SKIN

We know that smoking is a general bad boy and is singularly responsible for oh-so-many problems including cancer. But the way smoking slowly kills your appearance has to be seen to be believed. Smoking narrows the blood vessels in the outer layers of the skin which reduces the blood flow to the skin. When the blood flow to your skin is compromised, so is the supply of oxygen and nutrients to your skin causing early onset of wrinkles and early onset of ageing as a whole. Some smokers also appear pale and sometimes they have a lot of pigmentation on the face and body. You could be undoing all the advice in this book by smoking.

Of the mind-boggling 4,000 chemicals present in tobacco, several kick-start the destruction of collagen and elastin, which causes *permanent* wrinkles. Even hanging around smokers could age you. Passive smoking has been known to deteriorate the skin's building blocks. Smokers are also more susceptible to age spots, that is, spots of a darker colour on the face and the hands. Still want to light up?

Boozy lunches and dinners and night outs don't help your skin either. Alcohol is a prime cause of dehydration and we know that the drier our skin, the faster it ages. However, there are a few notable exceptions. Resveratrol, which is present in red wine, is a powerful antioxidant and therefore limited consumption of red wine is recommended for both your health and for your skin.

ESTABLISHING GOOD SKINCARE HABITS

If you add up the numbers, your total morning, day and night routine would barely total 10-15 minutes: 2-3 minutes in the morning, a few minutes applying and reapplying sunscreen during the day and about five minutes at night is all the daily investment you need for younger, better skin. Yet, changing habits are hard. Even the 10-15 minutes tacked on to a day marked by responsibilities, stress and deadlines seem too much. Here are some key methods that may help you better organize your time.

Don't set aside a separate time for your new skincare routine, especially for morning and evening care. Club the new skincare habits with existing habits. So, if you're brushing your teeth in the morning, add cleansing and moisturizing to something you already do. When you brush your teeth at night, add your five-minute night routine to it. When you're already in that zone, it's easy to add a few more things than to create a whole new regimen for it.

Accessibility is key to adaptability. Your sunscreen should be everywhere: in the bathroom, in your purse or backpack, in your office drawer, in your car. Instead of buying one big tube that you need to lug around and take with you wherever you go, buy three or four smaller tubes so you can apply or reapply when you get sixty seconds to yourself during the day. Also ensure that when you're running out of a moisturizer or night cream or cleanser, you go out and buy a new one before it gets over. If you always have access, it's easier to maintain good skin habits.

And lastly, when drinking water, drink as much as possible at one go. It is more convenient. Drinking a litre at one shot or four half-litre bottles is easier as opposed to eight or ten separate glasses that you have to remember to pour out and drink.

And we're nearly there. At the end of the chapter, that is. Don't worry about taking too many notes, though. As mentioned before, for your convenience, I have included at the end of this book age-specific beauty calendars. Each calendar contains a fully summarized skincare routine suited for your age band that will encapsulate not just this chapter but *all* key information in this book so that you're on the path to anti-ageing as soon as possible.

Did you know that under the outer layer of skin that you can see lies a whole world of glowing and fresh skin? Did you know that you could do a full body exfoliation with something as simple as a long bath and a towel? The second of the 5Es, Exfoliate, which is defined as the process of removing dead skin cells, is a detailed plan for weekly to monthly skincare that will discuss one of the most fundamental principles of skincare there is.

The Second 'E'. Exfoliate.
Because you are only as young as you Exfoliate.

The Onion

The starting point for exfoliation is, needless to say, the epidermis. And perhaps the simplest way to describe the epidermis is that it's like an onion. As we already know, with 15-20 layers of dead skin, the epidermis protects us from the world at large and is one of our first lines of defence. And this 'onion' naturally sheds layers of dead skin cells to reveal newer, younger skin underneath. Of the about 1.6 trillion skin cells that we have, we shed about a million dead cells every day.[6] To be replaced by new ones.

But as we also know, with age, cell turnover slows down. The onion takes longer to 'peel' itself. And just like the coarse, rough outer skin of the actual vegetable, the accumulation of useless dead skin cells can rob us of our youthful glow.

To look younger, we need to peel the onion. Ourselves.

Peeling the Onion

Exfoliation not only takes off the topmost layers of dead skin, it also gets rid of the build up of dirt, sebum (oil secreted by the sebaceous glands) and other germs and bacteria that are trapped in our pores. It doesn't help that we live in a hot and humid tropical country, where the need for deep scrubbing is vital.

Store shelves are packed with exfoliation solutions, from peels to scrubs to cleansers. There are also salons and clinics offering mechanical and chemical exfoliation

---

[6] Depending on your age.

treatments. You can't do peels every weekend or facials everyday. So what works well and when? And when is it safe to try these?

To understand what kind of exfoliation treatment works, we must go back to the analogy of the onion. Some treatments superficially peel the onion; some do a deeper, more thorough job of it. It's also never a good idea to peel the onion deeply all the time – that will only injure the skin. My experience of the last twenty years has taught me that there is a 'hierarchy' to exfoliation, and that every kind of exfoliation technique has a recommended time interval. I've mapped out the exfoliation hierarchy as follows and I've also added economical solutions wherever possible with ingredients that can be found in most Indian kitchens.

Peel away.

THE EXFOLIATION HIERARCHY

In the following, superficial exfoliation can be done once in about 7-10 days; medium-depth is best done once a month; while deep exfoliation should never be done *more* than once in 4-6 months.

SUPERFICIAL OR MECHANICAL EXFOLIATION (DIY)	Level *1*
MEDIUM-DEPTH OR SALON EXFOLIATION	Level *2*
DEEP OR MEDICAL EXFOLIATION	Level *3*

Also, if you have problem or sensitive skin or are undergoing treatment for any skin condition, this chapter is not for you. Unless otherwise specified by your doctor (sometimes exfoliation is recommended as part of ongoing acne treatment, for example), please stay away from *any* sort of exfoliating procedure, including the homemade ones. Because before you peel, you need to heal.

I
SUPERFICIAL OR MECHANICAL EXFOLIATION
FACTS

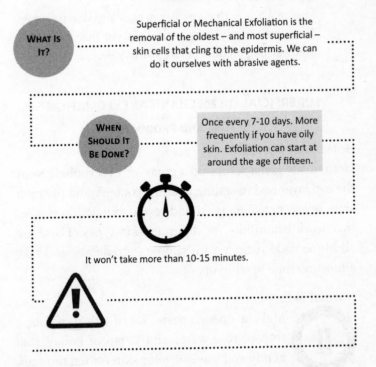

WHAT IS IT?
Superficial or Mechanical Exfoliation is the removal of the oldest – and most superficial – skin cells that cling to the epidermis. We can do it ourselves with abrasive agents.

WHEN SHOULD IT BE DONE?
Once every 7-10 days. More frequently if you have oily skin. Exfoliation can start at around the age of fifteen.

It won't take more than 10-15 minutes.

PROCEDURE

1. Moisten the skin. Never exfoliate dry skin.
2. Take a generous amount of the scrub or exfoliating product, layer it on your skin and gently rub in circular motions. Leave on as recommended. Unless otherwise indicated, if it dries before the time is up, moisten it again.
3. Wash off with water. Pat dry.
   Note:
   - Let whatever you're exfoliating with – whether it's a scrub or any other exfoliating medium – be the hero. In other words, let the product or scrub do the work. Gently apply and don't use pressure.
   - Also, make sure that you haven't got any skin treatment done immediately prior to the scrub, or that you haven't used a strong product before you exfoliate.

I
SUPERFICIAL OR MECHANICAL EXFOLIATION
SCRUBS AND PRODUCTS

HOMEMADE SCRUBS

Homemade facial scrubs do a great job of scrubbing away the top layer and revealing healthy, younger and plumper skin. Below are some tried-and-tested exfoliation classics that work beautifully for different skin types. These are all homemade recipes with simple ingredients, and take almost no time to whip up.

Normal Skin

Make a smooth paste out of 1 tbsp of oats, 1 tbsp of rose water and ½ tsp of honey. Rub gently and leave on your skin for ten minutes. Wash off with cold water and pat dry.

Dry Skin

d Make a paste out of 2 tbsps of honey (it's a humectant and helps to retain moisture), 2 tbsps of castor oil and 1 tbsp of crushed oats. Leave on for 5-7 minutes before washing off with water and patting dry. This scrub is very effective for dry skin.

Oily Skin

o 1. Take a medium-sized tomato and cut in half. Add 2 tbsps of sugar to a dish. Dip the cut side of the tomato into the sugar granules. Rub on wet skin for five minutes, followed by splashing cold water on the face. Pat dry with a towel. Tomato is rich in lycopene, a mighty anti-oxidant, and the sugar granules coax tomato to release more lycopene onto the skin, apart from also helping scrub the skin mechanically. It's a simple and brilliant scrub for oily skin.

2. A paste of ½ tsp of lime juice, 1 tsp sugar granules along with 1 to 1½ tsps of milk powder or multani mitti also works exceedingly well. Leave on for ten minutes before washing off.

3. And while we're on oily skin, let's not forget turmeric. Add ½ tsp of turmeric to 1 tbsp of honey and mix well. Apply on wet skin and leave on for five minutes. Rinse off with water. Rub your skin gently and complete the exfoliation process by applying ice on the face.

Combination or T-Zone Skin

T

For a good scrub for combination skin, mix 1 tsp of sugar (fine granules) with 1 tsp of oats. Add a little water and make a paste. Scrub your face, concentrating on the nose (T-zone) and the cheeks. After leaving on for 10-12 minutes, rinse it off gently in circular motions. Finish off by dabbing your skin with rose water and oil-free moisturizer.

Sensitive Skin

S

I'm afraid it's a myth that scrubs can be used on sensitive skin. Please check with your medical practitioner before using anything to exfoliate your skin. You may aggravate the problem.

Problem skin

P

Scrubs can't be used on problem skin either. Skin conditions like active acne, rosacea and so on should ideally never be subjected to scrubs. But check with your doctor.

Apart from the above, any face packs containing natural ingredients are great substitutes for scrubs. Egg yolk, honey, milk, aloe vera or essential oils are suited to dry skin while yogurt, egg white, fuller's earth, kaolin, gram flour, lemon, oats work well for oily skin and ripe sour fruit works beautifully for combination skin. These face packs not only exfoliate, but also brighten and smoothen the skin. See the box 'Pack It In' for some good, homemade face packs.

The bottom line is that for any good exfoliating home scrub, you need beneficial ingredients that suit your skin mixed with a substance that provides 'friction', like crushed apricot kernels, salt, sugar, orange peel powder, oatmeal or anything that acts as a 'tool', because it is the *abrasive* agent that gently removes the dead skin cells.

COMMERCIAL SCRUBS

Over The Counter (OTC) or commercially available scrubs that are indicated for your skin type work equally well. Do note that, unless otherwise specified, *all* commercially available scrubs and face packs will give you superficial exfoliation only. The key thing to remember here is that while you can follow the instructions on the pack, if you experience any irritation, stop immediately. And it's an absolute myth that the harder you scrub, the better the results. Relax, be gentle and enjoy the process.

PACK IT IN
HOMEMADE FACE PACKS

These homemade face packs can be used as a substitute for scrubs, and while each pack that I've recommended depends on your skin type, they all have the following steps in common:

Step 1: Before applying the pack, cleanse your face and pat dry.

Step 2: Apply the mask on your face.

Step 3: Put cold cotton dipped in rosewater on your eyes.

Step 4: After leaving the pack on for the recommended time, wash off with cold water. Pat dry.

Face pack for normal skin

Cut two cucumbers into cubes. To this, add half a cup of oats and make a coarse paste (which can be stored in the fridge for up to a week). Take 1 tbsp of this paste and add 1 tsp of milk cream (malai) to it. Leave on for ten minutes. Rinse off with cold water.

Face pack for dry skin

Mix 2 tbsps of milk powder and 2 tsps of honey with a few drops of water to make a smooth paste. If your skin is excessively dry, you can substitute water with a few drops of essential oil (rose or almond oil). Apply on your face and leave on for fifteen minutes.

Face pack for oily skin

Make a paste of 2tbsps of fuller's earth (multani mitti), 1 tsp of rosewater and a few drops of lime. Mix this well to make a smooth paste and apply on your face. Leave on for ten minutes and then wash off. Alternatively, you can make a paste of fuller's earth and mashed, overripe citrus fruit (like orange and sweet lime), which will work just as well.

Face pack for combination skin

Add a half cup of yogurt to one egg white and beat well. Apply on your face and leave on for fifteen minutes. Alternatively, combination skin also responds well to the mashed pulp of overripe fruit like bananas, strawberries, kiwi, papaya and the like. Mash the fruit thoroughly; add a few drops of honey or lime and apply on your face. You can leave it on for 10-12 minutes.

Face pack for sensitive and problem skin

If you have sensitive or problem skin, check with your doctor before applying anything to your face. If he or she is okay with you using a natural homemade face pack, you can start by making a powder of 2 tbsps of oats and 2 tsps of almonds. Add half a cucumber to this powder and blend in a blender. Leave this paste to cool in the fridge for 10-15 minutes and apply on your skin thereafter. Leave on for ten minutes and then wash off.

II
MEDIUM-DEPTH OR SALON EXFOLIATION
FACTS

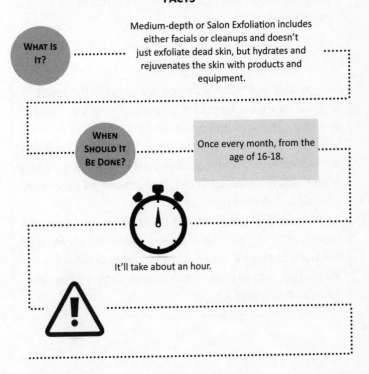

WHAT IS IT? .... Medium-depth or Salon Exfoliation includes either facials or cleanups and doesn't just exfoliate dead skin, but hydrates and rejuvenates the skin with products and equipment.

WHEN SHOULD IT BE DONE? .... Once every month, from the age of 16-18.

It'll take about an hour.

NOTE

1. Facials are best done in a salon by a trained professional. It's safer.
2. Facials don't work for all skin types. Sometimes standalone cleanups work better for those with sensitive skin or skin prone to acne. But if you do have problem or sensitive skin, check with your practitioner before you go in for a facial.
3. For a week before and after the facial or cleanup, avoid heat or laser treatment. Also give a miss to strong topical creams or even homemade skin solutions immediately before or after the treatment, unless otherwise indicated by your practitioner.

BLACK SHEEP

Believe it or not but blackheads are actually the result of a chain reaction. Hormonal changes make your body's sebaceous glands go into overdrive. These glands open up on your skin in the form of small pores. Sebum and dead skin cells collect in them causing comedones or whiteheads. When whiteheads are exposed to dirt, sunlight and pollution, they get oxidized and form blackheads.

Blackheads are embedded in the skin and are a little hard to remove by oneself. Commercially available blackhead strips will work to remove the ones that are already loose but it's always best to get a professional facial or cleanup, if possible, for a good, thorough job.

III
DEEP OR MEDICAL EXFOLIATION
FACTS

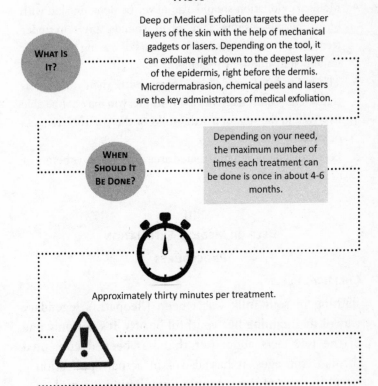

WHAT IS IT?

Deep or Medical Exfoliation targets the deeper layers of the skin with the help of mechanical gadgets or lasers. Depending on the tool, it can exfoliate right down to the deepest layer of the epidermis, right before the dermis. Microdermabrasion, chemical peels and lasers are the key administrators of medical exfoliation.

WHEN SHOULD IT BE DONE?

Depending on your need, the maximum number of times each treatment can be done is once in about 4-6 months.

Approximately thirty minutes per treatment.

NOTE

1. Medical exfoliation is not recommended for those younger than eighteen.

2. Choose your practitioner with care. These procedures could do more harm than help in the wrong hands.

3. For Asian skin types, this kind of exfoliation must never

target the dermis as that will trigger hyperpigmentation and an altogether new problem. Any deep exfoliation is for the epidermis only.

4. Medical exfoliation should also never be done on skin with burns, herpes, lesions, acne, open wounds, any skin under treatment or within twenty-four hours of waxing the area or immediately after any treatment.

5. These kinds of procedures come with their own post-treatment requirements and downtime: you may not be able to go out in the sun for a little while, or there may be redness or swelling.

6. Lastly, do not bleach the treated area until 7-10 days before or after the treatment.

III
DEEP OR MEDICAL EXFOLIATION
PROCEDURES

CHEMICAL PEELS

Bathing in sour milk was Queen Cleopatra's legendary way of maintaining her youthful beauty. It's not only one of the few facts about her that has been documented through the ages, it has also – in actual application – stood the test of time. At that time, bathing in milk may have been something that only the royalty did as a way of differentiating themselves from the rest and may have been used for moisturizing or cleansing, but we now know that lactic acid in milk *exfoliates* dead skin as well as brightening it and aiding mild collagen synthesis.

Chemical exfoliation removes the skin's outer layers with the help of chemicals. It also works beautifully to minimize the appearance of fine lines and enhance skin texture. Common chemical peels include:

a. **Peels with AHAs (Alpha Hydroxy Acids)**

AHAs loosen dead skin cells, enabling them to turn over quickly. Lactic acid(derived from milk), glycolic acid (derived from sugarcane) and malic acid (derived from apple) are common AHA peels. Glycolic and lactic acids both stimulate collagen synthesis. And while glycolic acid is the most widely used AHA peel, lactic acid is milder and not as irritating to the skin.

b. **Peels with BHAs (Beta Hydroxy Acids)**

In BHA peels, salicylic acid peels are the most common. This peel is designed to dissolve the stratum corneum – the outermost dead skin layer – layer by layer revealing a whole new you. These kinds of peels are best suited for oily skin types.

c. **Peels with Retinol**

Retinol is an excellent exfoliating agent with antioxidant as well as moisturizing properties. It helps increase cell turnover, disperses the melanin pigment and aids collagen synthesis.

d. **Peels with Enzymes**

The peel derived from the Papain enzyme found in papaya cleanses pores, improves skin tone as well as smoothens skin texture. Additionally, there is no injury to live cells when it is used; it removes only the dead ones.

e. **TCA peels** (trichloro-acetic acid peel)

TCA peels are medium-depth peels, which can be used for fine lines, acne scars, pigmentation and to help improve general skin tone and texture. It comes in different levels or 'strengths' – 15, 25, 50 and even 100 per cent. TCA peels loosen the bonds of dead skin surface cells and stimulate the repair of the skin. Sun protection is strictly advised after treatment. While it does give excellent results when done with caution – and by an experienced expert – these kinds of peels are not recommended for Asian skin types, with the exception of cases of acne scars.

f. **Phenol peels**

This is one of the deepest peels that exist and causes the maximum level of exfoliation. Not only is it done under the supervision of an experienced dermatologist, it is also always done under anaesthesia. Phenol peels, though, are not recommended for Asian skin because there's a high possibility of scarring and post-treatment pigmentation, which could even end up being permanent.

While it's best to ask your doctor or practitioner for advice on which peel to go for, remember that there are so many peels that have been derived from nature and from what is already and abundantly all around us.

MICRODERMABRASION

When I first started learning microdermabrasion, I went to Munich for my training. And came back to India more confused than when I started because all training for microdermabrasion at that time was designed for

Caucasian skin. And while I had great belief in the process, I was anxious to ensure that it beautified our Indian skin effectively. I kept adjusting the settings on the equipment, made my own mistakes – mostly on myself – and learnt through experience until we finally perfected the protocols for our skin.

Microdermabrasion can be a superficial exfoliation procedure administered by a trained aesthetician. But it can also be a deeper kind of exfoliation if a doctor – with the help of a diamond-tipped wheel or wand to abrade and smoothen the skin – performs the treatment. The science behind the medical procedure is to injure the skin so that old cells pave the way for the formation of new skin cells. The more pressure applied, the deeper the exfoliation. Microdermabrasion can also cause a little redness and swelling post the procedure, but that's temporary. New skin growth should occur in about 5-8 days and it's also great for the removal of plaque and 'skin debris'.

Diana Hayden, Miss World 1997, is a firm believer in microdermabrasion and books a session with me whenever she thinks her skin is looking dull, tired or feeling rough. A great believer of exfoliation, when she was researching material for her book, *A Beautiful Truth*, she was a happy woman because the one thing she believed the most in was reinforced again and again in her research – that exfoliation was definitely crucial for exquisite skin. She was doing it right all along. She says she emerges from the process with her skin sloughed off, leaving her face feeling 'super clean and rejuvenated'. I'll second that.

ABLATIVE LASERS

Ablative laser resurfacing uses laser technology to remove the upper, thinner layers of the skin. It is a deep, aggressive form of exfoliation. Due to the nature of the treatment, the recovery time may be longer than other deep exfoliation treatments. Discomfort, swelling and redness may occur briefly afterwards, but it also works beautifully.

After reading all of this, are you scratching your head, wondering which one's the best treatment option for you? Well, I'll have to look at your skin to tell you that. In short, depending on the degree of exfoliation – light or deep – and what your skin additionally needs, it's best to ask your doctor or the practitioner examining you for advice on which peel or treatment to get. What I can tell you is that deep exfoliation is one of the most popular celeb treatments, which is an indication of both its popularity and its efficacy.

There is an exfoliating product or an ingredient for everyone. But don't exfoliate too often or too hard. It also irritates the skin when you choose products with harsh ingredients. At the risk of repeating myself, avoid excess sun exposure after some of these procedures and don't forget to ask your doctor about the downtime and recovery period. It's crucial – both for your health and for the success of the procedure.

Skin cell debris is constantly forming day and night, twenty-four hours a day, 365 days a year. If you come to me one day and ask me to give you the three magic words that would unlock the gates to fantastic skincare, I'd say

IT'S SLOUGH OR NEVER
BODY EXFOLIATION IDEAS

Why deprive the rest of your body of the goodness of exfoliation? Here are some tips that really work:

1. **For full body exfoliation**

   I was in Turkey sometime back and nobody should leave the place without experiencing their famous exfoliating 'hamaam bath'. The luxury of it – even though I felt the 'loofah' was being rubbed too hard – was difficult to forget and my skin glowed and glowed for *weeks*. If you can get the skin 'loofahed' this extensively and thoroughly, then once a month would be great for a full-body exfoliation. Alternatively, you could also exfoliate with a towel. Towel exfoliation works best after soaking the body's skin for a while in a pool of water (in the bathtub or a swimming pool). After emerging, rub your body vigorously with a towel. Dead skin cells get exfoliated beautifully. Never forget to apply a nice body lotion or cream to finish.

2. **For elbows and knees**

   Elbow skin and knee skin tend to be drier and darker than the rest of the body due to sun exposure, heredity, or even constant friction due to continuous surface contact. Exfoliation can brighten and smoothen knees and elbows. Try gentle exfoliating scrubs, followed by deep moisturizing agents. If the condition is severe, a skin brightening chemical peel or a bleach applied to that area also works.

3. **For feet**

   Add the juice of half a lemon to warm water and soak your feet in it for about ten minutes. Take your feet out of the water and rub off dead skin cells with a pumice stone. Lemon is a mild and natural acid that works to dissolve dead and dry skin for easy removal.

that actually it's one magic word repeated three times: Exfoliate. Exfoliate. Exfoliate. This is one of skincare's most fundamental lessons.

When you have dead skin debris, your skin doesn't reflect light. The moment you exfoliate, your skin reflects light and that's why you glow. Of all the beautification treatments that exist, exfoliation is perhaps one of the most effective and subtle things you can do to your face and body. It makes a world of difference and no one can quite put their finger on what is different about you. Because exfoliation done well is quite literally a whole new face.

Did you know that simply protecting yourself against the sun can dramatically lessen the incidence of pigmentation? Did you know that the light-handed, 'less is more' approach works best even for heavy acne and deep wrinkles? The third E, Erase, will talk about some common skin problems and what you can do about them.

The Third 'E'. Erase.
Because, sometimes, you are only as young as you Erase.

What's bothering you? A fine line? A wrinkle? A deep groove? A dark spot? Acne that never seems to go away? In this, the third E, we will talk about common skin problems as well as the deeper lines and furrows that I have been treating for the last twenty years. The first two Es, Everyday and Exfoliation, are as anti-ageing as they are – in many cases – *preventive*, designed to delay ageing for as long as possible. Erase is *reactive*. When spots or acne show up for no apparent reason or when furrows become deeper and deeper due to the passage of time, Erase will show you how to deal with skin conditions that have presented themselves without invitation on your face or body and what you can do about it.

Everybody wants smoother, tighter and younger skin. Erase will talk about the three roadblocks to this by dividing the chapter into three parts.

Erase Acne

Erase Spots

Erase Lines

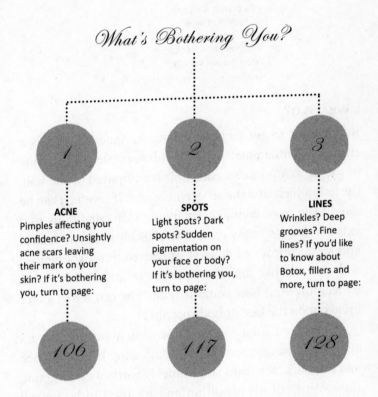

What's Bothering You?

1

ACNE
Pimples affecting your confidence? Unsightly acne scars leaving their mark on your skin? If it's bothering you, turn to page:

106

2

SPOTS
Light spots? Dark spots? Sudden pigmentation on your face or body? If it's bothering you, turn to page:

117

3

LINES
Wrinkles? Deep grooves? Fine lines? If you'd like to know about Botox, fillers and more, turn to page:

128

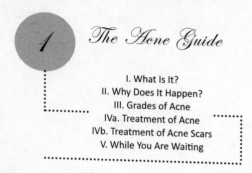

The Acne Guide

I. WHAT IS IT?

If you want to get technical about it, Acne Vulgaris is a chronic and inflammatory disease of the pilosebaceous units of the skin. A pilosebaceous unit is composed of the hair, the hair follicle and the sebaceous gland. If severe, it can be one of the most confidence-zapping skin conditions that exist. In fact, in many cases, the emotional, psychological and social impact of acne is similar to that experienced with diseases like diabetes, epilepsy or arthritis. It makes us feel low. And how could it not? How can a big, angry breakout on the face or body *not* affect you?

It bothered John Abraham for sure. About 10-12 years ago, he had severe acne that was affecting his confidence and his work. My team and I quickly worked on targeting the severity of his condition and we used to be on-call 24×7 for any emergencies if the acne recurred for any reason or if there was a shoot coming up. We finished the treatment by eliminating the scars that severe acne has a dirty tendency of leaving behind.

A case of severe acne was one of my first big cases in the first year of my practice. Roma's pimples were as big as peas, full of pus and all over her face. Her acne was merciless; I could barely see her skin. She was in tears. Not just from the severity of her condition, but also because I was her last resort.

She had other symptoms as well. Upon further examination, I observed that she had more hair than normal on her chin and upper lip; she had dark, hard hair on her legs; the hair on her head was thinning; she had an oily scalp and the ends of her hair were dry. She also had dark body folds and a bunch of hard hair in the umbilical line. To me, all this screamed of irregular hormone levels. I told her to get a blood test and a sonography done. It was just as I had suspected. She had severe Polycystic Ovarian Syndrome or PCOS.

II. WHY DOES ACNE HAPPEN?

Acne rears its pimply head either due to the fact that you are genetically predisposed to it, or because your body is going through some sort of hormonal tsunami like it does during puberty and adolescence or during certain hormone-imbalancing conditions like pregnancy, menopause and PCOS. Certain medications like drugs with corticosteroids, androgens or lithium can also cause acne. The following triggers can aggravate an existing bout of acne, but are *not* the root cause of it:

- Stress
- Irregular sleeping patterns and unsuitable food intake including foods high in sugar and fat
- Unsuitable skin products or changing skincare products too often

- Bad skin habits like pinching or pressing pimples
- Waxing facial hair
- Sleeping without removing make-up
- Excessive use of products with active ingredients in high concentration
- Forcibly extricating blackheads or whiteheads
- Allergic reactions
- Going to unhygienic places for cleanups

When I started Blush, I knew I could treat acne with medicines, but in some cases, pustular acne had to be cut open and blackheads had to be manually extracted through a cleanup. It was a very delicate and sensitive procedure and had to be done extremely cautiously. To ensure that we maintained the stringent standards Blush is known for, I personally trained all my staff in the way I wanted it to be done, and before any new girl worked on any client, I made sure she did the treatment on me. The touch, the movement, the rhythm all had to be the same as mine. Don't handover your trust on a plate to people and places that haven't made a commitment to basic cleanliness. It's one of the worst things you can do to yourself.

III. GRADES OF ACNE

Treatment for acne depends on the severity of the condition. Do note that apart from the face, acne can sometimes appear just on the nose or also on the neck, upper arms, back and chest. Depending on the extent of the breakout, acne can be graded as:

Mild

Mild Acne

- Here, about one fourth of the face is affected.
- Mild acne characterized by few to several papules or pustules, but no nodules or scarring.

Moderate

Moderate Acne

- About half the face is affected.
- Mild acne characterized by several to many papules or pustules and a few to several nodules.
- Additionally, a few scars may also be present.

Severe

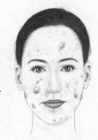

Severe Acne

- In severe acne, you can see multiple papules or pustules and many nodules. Scarring is often present.
- In many cases, about three-quarters of the face is affected.

IVa. TREATMENT OF ACNE

Acne, unfortunately, cannot just be treated and forgotten. As a farewell present, it could leave behind mild to deep, pitted scars. Comprehensive treatment for this condition is always three-fold and has the following objectives:

1. To prevent new outbursts of acne
2. To heal the existing acne

3. To prevent, minimize and remove the scars it leaves behind

Below is a range of solutions for acne treatment. This will take care of (1) and (2) mentioned in the above list.

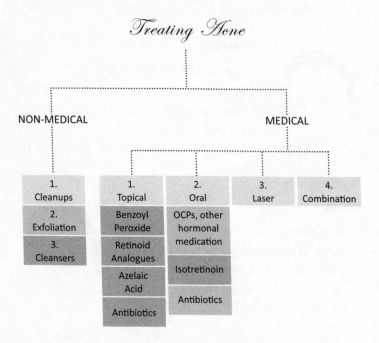

Treating Acne

NON-MEDICAL	MEDICAL			
1. Cleanups	1. Topical	2. Oral	3. Laser	4. Combination
2. Exfoliation	Benzoyl Peroxide	OCPs, other hormonal medication		
3. Cleansers	Retinoid Analogues			
	Azelaic Acid	Isotretinoin		
	Antibiotics	Antibiotics		

As you can see, it's quite a list. To truly, thoroughly see the back of your acne outburst, depending on the severity of the condition, standard lines of treatment for acne include:

a. **Cleanups, cleansing and very mild exfoliation**. To remove excess oil and dead skin cells. Exfoliation cannot be done on active acne but on the oily skin where there is a build up of dead skin cells.

b. **Topical applications**. Antibiotic gels like clindamycin work well on mild to moderate acne. These can be used along with topical retinoids, benzoyl peroxide or azelaic acid to unclog the pores.

c. **Mild oral antibiotics**. Used for moderate to severe acne with the objective of reducing bacteria on the skin, thereby reducing acne.

d. **Oral Contraceptive Pills or OCPs**. To address hormonal imbalances in women.

e. **Isotretinoin**. By itself or along with mild antibiotics or hormonal pills.

f. **Lasers**. Lasers and light therapies target bacteria that cause acne inflammation and reduce active acne.

We've also used soft gel peels containing salicylic acid and mandelic acid to reduce acne-causing bacteria. Cryotherapy also works well to reduce inflammatory acne. Further, if you're female and reading this, *don't* be resistant to going on hormone pills. It works beautifully to both arrest and reverse acne and then can be weaned off when not needed. Roma, even with her severe acne, had to be convinced to go on a mild oral hormone pill after she did her tests and had confirmed her PCOS diagnosis with her gynaecologist. But after the combination treatment plan – that had to be checked for contraindications – included gel-based peels and topical creams, she was amazed and delighted with the results.

IVb. Treatment of Acne Scars

Depending on the case, acne can leave behind not one, not two, but *three* different kinds of scars:

1. **Flat marks**. Flat red or brown spots.
2. **Pitted scars**. Depressed areas or small craters or indentations. Pitted scars are additionally divided into ice pick, box car and rolling scars. Ice pick scars go deep into the skin but on the surface look like tiny openings, as if pricked by a sharp object. Box car scars are wider, broader and run deeper than ice pick scars and also have more well-defined edges. Rolling scars have a wave-like appearance; they are broader, continuous scars, almost like a group of scars together.
3. **Keloid scars**. These are raised, bumpy scars and hardened scars visible especially on those patients with keloid tendencies, which we will go into further detail later in this book.

Below is a spectrum of solutions to treat different kinds of acne scars:

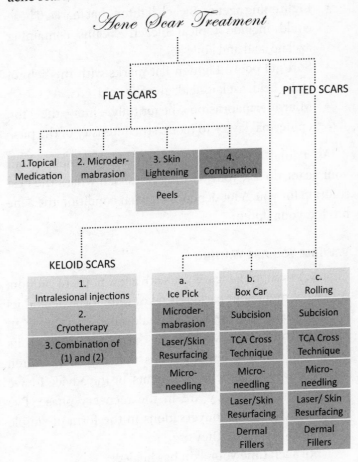

Acne Scar Treatment

FLAT SCARS — PITTED SCARS

1.Topical Medication	2. Microdermabrasion	3. Skin Lightening	4. Combination
		Peels	

KELOID SCARS

| 1. Intralesional injections |
| 2. Cryotherapy |
| 3. Combination of (1) and (2) |

a. Ice Pick	b. Box Car	c. Rolling
Microdermabrasion	Subcision	Subcision
Laser/Skin Resurfacing	TCA Cross Technique	TCA Cross Technique
Microneedling	Microneedling	Microneedling
	Laser/Skin Resurfacing	Laser/Skin Resurfacing
	Dermal Fillers	Dermal Fillers

As you can see, the treatment is quite intricate. To elaborate on a few tools used:

- **Lightening agents**. Bleach lightens flat marks. These could include topical bleach creams containing azelaic acid and kojic acid.
- **Soft gel peels**. Lighten flat marks with the help of lactic acid, azelaic acid, glycolic acid, etc.
- **Microdermabrasion** beautifully lifts the top epidermal layers to reduce the intensity of the pits.

As a final note, when it comes to smoothening out your scars, do ask your treating physician what's the best solution for you. A lot depends on what condition the acne has left your skin in.

V. While You Are Waiting

Finally, I thought I'd leave you with a few notes of caution. As we chatted about earlier, it takes time for acne and its scars to leave your system. It could take weeks or even months while you're waiting for the treatment to do its work. I've noted a few questions that my clients often ask me during their acne treatments, or the advice I have given them while they are in the recovery phase. I've reproduced lengthy conversations in the form of simple Dos and Don'ts. Here they are.

Until such time your skin has healed:

DON'T

- Use anything harsh on your skin. Ideally, you shouldn't be doing this anyway but even more so during your recovery from acne.

- Squeeze pimples. Which, again, ideally, you should never do anyway, acne or no acne.
- Exfoliate. Until otherwise specified by your doctor.
- Buy or use OTC products without asking your doctor.
- Wax facial, chest and back hair, as it could lead to further breakouts.
- Use too much of topical medication, even if it has been prescribed by your physician. Even when it comes to acne treatment, less is always more. Use the medicine as sparingly as possible or as indicated by your treating doctor. Ensure that there is no misunderstanding between the two of you about the exact quantity that needs to be used.
- Use a rough towel to dry the face.

DO
- Use sunscreen religiously, twice a day. It doesn't matter whether it's winter, summer or the monsoon or if you have sand, snow or water around you.
- Keep your skin clean.
- Drink more water than you usually do.
- Use salicylic acid face washes or those that are mild and suited to your skin.
- Remove all make-up before you hit the sack.

The above will, with very few exceptions and with the help of your doctor, ensure that your acne is treated and you look like your old self again. Cleanliness and hygiene, lifestyle and dietary adjustments, awareness and regular follow-ups with the doctor will go a long way in making sure your skin gets back its glow again.

Apart from at the time of puberty, acne can happen anytime and anywhere. Male or female, if you're reading this because you want to solve your acne problem, you are not alone. With very few exceptions, acne is definitely the symptom of *something* going on inside your body so it's always best to understand the reason by seeking medical help instead of self-medicating and worsening the problem. While it is widely prevalent, it is precisely *because* of this wide prevalence that there are lots of doctors with lots of experience at treating this with lots of tools at their disposal. Do note that while acne treatment can sometimes take time, it's very, very important that you don't lose heart because smooth, beautiful, glorious skin is waiting for you on the other side.

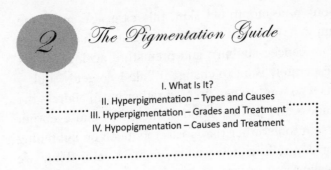

I. What Is It

I will never forget the most extraordinary client I have ever had. She refused to make eye contact. She cried while I was talking. She was least interested in what I was saying and, at one unforgettable point, started to drool all over her pretty little dress.

She was nine months old.

When Sharbani and her husband, Manek, came in with a baby all bundled up, I thought that the client – like any other doctor would have thought – was one of the parents. They walked in, sat down, unwrapped their precious little bundle and asked me, very seriously, if there was something I could do to make their nine-month-old baby *fairer*. They were very concerned about her skin colour and thought that if they started early, they would be able to maintain her complexion over time. Or at least prevent it from darkening further.

Even for a fairness-obsessed society like ours, this was one of the most unusual lightening requests I had ever received, and here I thought I had seen it all. While I turned the 'client' away and refused to treat her soft, precious nine-month-old skin, this case also made me unhappy. It is sad that the very pigment that protects us from cancer, sunburn and premature ageing is what we desperately want to change. While I do get – adult – clients who want to be fairer, I'd rather try to address the patchiness and pigmentation of their skin and even out their skin tone rather than focus too much on lightening it. Our skin reflects how we live, what we eat and how we are feeling and as long as it is healthy and is reflecting light, it is beautiful.

In this section you will find your guide to pigmentation and what you can do about it. When I refer to pigmentation, I'm talking about spots or patches or discolouration of the skin. If the discolouration is lighter than the skin tone, it's called *hypo*pigmentation and if it's darker than the skin tone, it's called *hyper*pigmentation. I usually treat the more common hyperpigmentation or dark spots/patches, even though we will briefly discuss both dark and light discolouration.

II. HYPERPIGMENTATION – TYPES AND CAUSES

Hyperpigmentation occurs when there is an overproduction of the melanin pigment. In my practice, I find that for every 10 cases of pigmentation I treat, nine are suffering from hyperpigmentation while only one has hypopigmentation. It's relatively common, relatively harmless but has been known to distress and deeply affect the people who have it. While hyperpigmentation can strike anywhere on your body, it usually sets up camp on the face or on the arms.

Common types of hyperpigmentation include:

1. **Lentigo or lentigenes**. These are freckles. Lentigo refers to one freckle; lentigenes refer to multiple freckles. These are usually light brown, most commonly appear on the face and neck, usually occur in the teens and are an inherited condition.

2. **Melasma**. Often nicknamed the 'pregnancy mask', melasma is triggered by hormonal changes brought on by pregnancy and are pigmented splotches found usually on the face (except the eye area). By and large, both sides of the face are affected. Melasma is most commonly found on the cheeks, the forehead, the bridge of the nose and the upper lip.

3. **Solar lentigens**. Also called 'age spots' or 'liver spots', these are usually caused by sun damage. Age spots look quite similar to freckles and while these are generally found on the hands and the face, any area exposed to the sun can be affected to include the shoulders, neck and the back of the hands. This kind of hyperpigmentation is usually seen in people over the age of forty.

Additionally, in many cases, there are patches on the body that are darker than the rest of the skin to include darker skin on the nape of the neck, underarms and even the skin on the inner thighs, which is caused either due to friction – in cases of obesity – or even due to hormonal changes. Appropriate brightening treatments are carried out on a case-to-case basis with a view to merging the darkened patch with the rest of the skin.

DARK CIRCLES

Dark circles – or peri-orbital darkening – appear when haemoglobin oxidizes; in other words, when your capillaries 'leak' blood. And while it's possible that your capillaries are leaking blood in other parts of your body, skin around the eyes being delicate and thin, this leakage shows up in the form of dark circles.

While lack of refreshing sleep or sleeping late, unhealthy eating, inadequate consumption of water, staring at computer screens or TV screens for hours and hours, not wearing your spectacles (if prescribed), low haemoglobin levels and stress all lead to this condition, genes are the *biggest* culprit. If you're prone to dark circles, it could be because they run in your family.

Creams with lightening agents like Vitamin C, kojic acid, arbutin and azelaic acid put up a fight against dark circles and work well to combat them. Apply the cream on the affected area and leave on overnight to greatly lighten the circles over time. Take a look at *Express* for quick, homemade solutions.

Causes

Why does it happen? What makes spots and splotches suddenly spring up from nowhere? The primary causes of hyperpigmentation include:

- **Sun exposure**. Year-round exposure to the sun's rays stimulates the overproduction of melanin.
- **Hormonal imbalances,** which occur during pregnancy, post-pregnancy, peri-menopause or menopause.
- Antibiotics, hormone treatments, anti-seizure or anti-malarial **drugs**, all of which can bring on hyperpigmentation.

- Certain **diseases** like Addison's disease and hypothyroidism, which are also known to cause hyperpigmentation.
- **Skin injuries** and inflammation. Injury could lead to PIH or Post-inflammatory Hyperpigmentation. Even a relatively simple problem like a mosquito bite can cause PIH.

III. HYPERPIGMENTATION – GRADES AND TREATMENT

Grades

Based on what caused it and where it's located on the skin's surface, hyperpigmentation is broadly classified into three grades:

1. **Epidermal pigmentation**. This is a relatively easier grade of pigmentation to treat as it is close to the surface of the skin and is usually caused due to sun exposure. Freckles would fall under this grade.

2. **Dermal pigmentation**. This grade of pigmentation is found deeper in the skin, in the dermal layer, as the name suggests. Because it's deeper, it's also harder to treat.

3. **Mixed dermal/epidermal pigmentation**. Melasma is a classic example of this grade of pigmentation, where it is present both on the dermal layer as well as the epidermal layer.

Standard Treatment for Hyperpigmentation

First, the bad news. Hyperpigmentation cannot be completely erased. But don't lose hope and don't put down the book yet. Hyperpigmentation can be brilliantly *lightened*, which would enable it to be further concealed by make-up. Keep reading the treatments for hyperpigmentation:

1. **Topical creams with lightening agents**. These creams work by hampering the production of melanin while simultaneously increasing cell turnover by sloughing off the top layer of dead skin so that the existing pigmentation is flushed out. The best topical creams for hyperpigmentation are:

   a. **Kojic acid**. It is a very popular lightening agent, also found in night repair creams, moisturizers and more. It prevents the production of melanin.

   b. **Azelaic acid**. Brimming with anti-bacterial properties, azelaic acid was primarily used to treat acne but was accidentally found to possess skin-lightening properties and, since 2007, is also widely used to treat sun spots and pigmentation.

   c. **Mandelic acid**. This agent has anti-bacterial properties and works to slough off the top layer of dead skin cells, enabling faster cell turnover. The healthier cells revealed underneath are also lighter in comparison to the more hyperpigmented layer.

   d. **Hydroquinone**. This is a very effective lightening agent but it makes the skin sensitive on application and therefore cannot be subjected to prolonged sun exposure – as it can cause skin irritation and PIH – which makes it difficult for Indians or anyone living in tropical countries to implement. Which is why hydroquinone treatment is not recommended in India.

Further, note that only qualified practitioners should prescribe these creams. I strongly recommend that you do not self-medicate because dosage is very important. Like with most of the advice in this book, *less is more* with these creams as well. If used in excess, they irritate the skin and not only cause redness but could also worsen the pigmentation by over-sensitizing the skin even before the results are seen.

2. **Protection from the sun**. Wearing at least SPF 15 sunscreen every four hours and restricting sun exposure is crucial in containing and preventing hyperpigmentation.

3. **Early action**. In the initial stages of pigmentation, home remedies work well to stall the progress of the pigmentation. To make a skin-brightening mask, take the juice of half a lime and mix it with the juice of half a medium-sized potato (grate to remove the juice). Lime is rich in citric acid and therefore helps to bleach the skin while potatoes contain the catecholase enzyme, which also helps brighten the skin.

4. **Exfoliate regularly**. The piling up of dead skin cells further aggravates discolouration and pigmentation. So ensure that you exfoliate regularly. However, choose extremely mild exfoliants and light peels as opposed to stronger products. If the products are too intense, the skin gets damaged and subsequent sun exposure could actually worsen hyperpigmentation and defeat the whole point of exfoliation in the first place.

LASER TREATMENT FOR HYPERPIGMENTATION

Lasers are attracted to melanin. How it works is that the melanin absorbs the laser light, heat is generated and the darker cells that are being targeted are destroyed, and the pigmentation is lightened as a result. Generally, the wavelengths that are attracted to the melanin in pigmented lesions range from 532 nanometers(nm) to 1064nm and at these wavelengths, the laser leaves the surrounding skin unaffected in a process called selective photothermolysis.

Theoretically, it sounds fail-proof but the success of the laser to treat hyperpigmnetation depends greatly on the depth of the melanin and the colour of the lesion. Results are, to put it simply, unpredictable. Though all these devices work, it is important to have an in-depth analysis of the pigmentation of your skin to determine what will be right for you. Lasers work better for Caucasian skin but in us Indians, I've seen that the laser treatment mostly

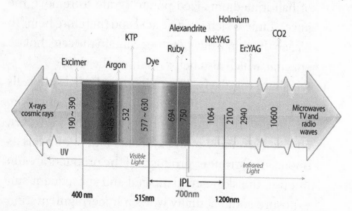

Source: http://www.adarecosmetics.ie/news/lasers-what-are-they-and-what-do-they-do

aggravates the problem after an initial sign of improvement. Even so, while some lesions do not disappear completely, they will be significantly lighter in colour after treatment. There are some post-treatment requirements like sun protection and topical applications. If you feel that this is something you want to do, then do some further research and schedule an in-depth conversation with your doctor.

IV. HYPOPIGMENTATION – GRADES AND TREATMENT

While it doesn't occur as rampantly as hyperpigmentation, listed below are some key types of hypopigmentation.

1. **Polymorphous Light Eruption (PLE).** PLE appears in the form of white patches on the skin, especially on the faces of children due to excess sun exposure. Worried parents often mistake PLE for a fungal infection. PLE is also seen in people with outdoor jobs or who spend a significant amount of time out in the sun like sportspeople.

2. **Deficiencies of vitamins B, C and D** and **calcium** can trigger hypopigmentation.

3. **Post injury (PIH – Post Inflammatory Hypopigmentation).** Post-injury skin discolouration could greatly contribute to hypopigmentation. The thing to note here is that it is not permanent, though it may take a long time to re-pigment.

4. **Albinism.** Albinism is a rare, genetic disorder where the enzyme that produces melanin is absent. This leads to a total lack of pigmentation in the skin, hair or eyes.

IT'S A STRETCH

Stretch marks occur when the elastic and collagen fibres in your skin permanently snap, which could be due to sudden weight gain or loss or even possibly due to severe torsion of the skin during certain kinds of 'twisting' exercises. Although your skin is pretty elastic, the normal production of collagen is disrupted when it is overstretched, leading to stretch marks. Now, whether you form these marks or not depend on how elastic the elastin fibres in the dermal layer of your skin are, and that is something I believe is hereditary.

Instead of stretching this particular story out, let me get to the point: getting completely rid of stretch marks may not be possible. Because once the elasticity of your skin is hampered, it is difficult to repair. But stretch marks *can* be reduced by topical creams that contain Retino A or other derivatives of Vitamin A as this vitamin has the ability to stimulate collagen synthesis and especially work when your stretch marks are in the beginning stages and appear red or purplish. In other words, tackling them early on with creams and other techniques is key. Laser therapy may also help: laser light can break down scar tissue and bring about the repair of elastin and aid in the production of collagen. You can lessen their intensity, yes, but it's a bit of a stretch to think that you can make them completely disappear.

5. **Pityriasis Alba.** This is seen mostly in children and is characterized by colourless, scaly skin patches.
6. **Vitiligo** is one of the most challenging forms of hypopigmentation and is an autoimmune disorder in which the pigment-producing cells are damaged. Though genetic, it's not contagious but

does, unfortunately, have a stigma attached to it. Combination treatments work well in the initial stages.

Self-medication is a big no-no for hypopigmentation and should only be done under the watchful eye of a qualified physician. Treatment options for this condition include topical corticosteroids or tars (topical cream), light/laser treatment or surgical skin grafting.

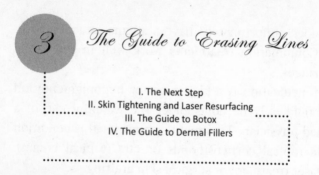

3 The Guide to Erasing Lines

I. The Next Step
II. Skin Tightening and Laser Resurfacing
III. The Guide to Botox
IV. The Guide to Dermal Fillers

I. THE NEXT STEP

When fat pads start to go south, bone starts to resorb, the skin starts to sag and parts of our faces start to visibly show signs of more advanced ageing, even the best cream or exfoliation technique will not be able to help you. Topical treatments work well in the initial stages of ageing and are great to delay ageing for as long as possible. But, in case of severe volume or fat loss on the face, they are not going to help. The Guide to Erasing Lines is about the next level of skincare. Whether you want to take up that next level is entirely up to you.

Do remember that any foray into Botox or fillers or other injectibles must be accompanied by a holistic regimen of skincare. Do your night care routine, exfoliate regularly, drink more water, sleep better, make adjustments to your lifestyle. It will not only complement the procedure that you have done but since injectibles target only specific areas, you need to take care of the rest of your skin as well. And since many skincare recommendations work wonderfully for the rest of your body, you really have nothing to lose.

GRADING OF WRINKLES

Wrinkles are of two types: fine surface lines and deep furrows. The furrows can be further classified as dynamic or static lines. Dynamic lines only appear on movement/expression (squinting/frowning) of the muscle, that is, when you frown, smile, show anger, etc. Static lines are those that remain unchanged with muscle movement; for example, the presence of crow's feet around the eyes irrespective of whether you are crinkling your eyes or not.

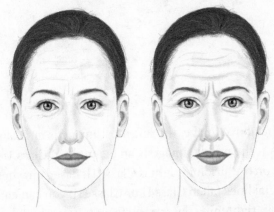

Static and Dynamic Lines: On the left are static lines, which are visible when your face is at rest. Dynamic lines, on the right, are lines that appear on movement and expression. Over time, dynamic lines can become deeper static lines.

The Fitzpatrick classification of facial lines essentially refers to how much wrinkling is seen around the eyes and the mouth.[7]

[7] 'Facial Lines and Wrinkles', accessed 30 December 2014, http://dermnetnz.org/site-age-specific/wrinkles.html.

Class I is characterized by fine wrinkles.

Class II is characterized by fine-to-moderately deep wrinkles and a moderate number of lines.

Class III is characterized by fine-to-deep wrinkles, multiple lines as well as possibly redundant folds.

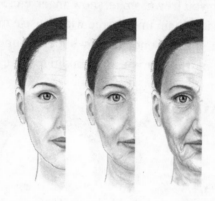

In the above image, the left most image is an example of Class I, the middle image is an example of Class II and the one on the absolute right is Class III. Based on whether your facial lines fall in Class II or Class III, you can choose from skin tightening, laser resurfacing, Botox and dermal filler treatments.

II. SKIN TIGHTENING AND LASER RESURFACING

Laser resurfacing uses a laser to strip the uppermost layers of the skin to reduce the appearance of wrinkles, lines and sun damage on the uppermost layers, especially around the eyes, mouth and cheeks. Depending on your skin and your requirements, either one of the following can work:

1. A wounding (ablative) laser, which removes thin layers of skin.
2. A non-wounding (non-ablative) laser, which works at a deeper level of the epidermis.

The skin can take a couple of weeks to heal after the treatment, depending on the type and extent of the treatment. Non-ablative treatments tend to heal a bit faster. Note, however, that laser resurfacing treatments cannot eliminate deep furrows or sagging skin.

There are also radiofrequency treatments for skin firming where penetration of the radio frequency waves deep into the dermis regenerate and contract collagen, gradually decreasing wrinkles.

Additionally, the heat generated during this treatment activates the fibroblasts and produces more new collagen and elastin fibres enabling skin tightening for a longer duration. Which is why the results – while taking their time to appear in 2-6 months – usually last upto a year.

III. THE GUIDE TO BOTOX

Dubbed the 'miracle wrinkle remover' of the century, Botox is the brand name of a neuromodulator made from the Botulinum toxin, which, on injecting, relaxes the muscle and therefore the wrinkle, leading to a smoother and more youthful appearance. I deeply believed in its potential and I was waiting to bring it to the Indian market, which I eventually did in the year 2000. Originally used for medical and neurological – and not cosmetic – purposes, it is *the* number one cosmetic procedure in the world today and it has – over a fifteen-year period of usage – treated thousands of my clients and has earned every bit of its formidable reputation.

Botox works by briefly blocking the signals from the nerves to the muscles, thus reducing muscle movement which softens and relaxes wrinkles. It works quickly and you can see results within 3-7 days and it can last anywhere between 3-6 months. It doesn't take much time to implement either–about 10-15 minutes in the clinic, which is why it is called a lunch-time procedure. Botox has *no* recovery time.

The flip side to it is that treatments must be repeated every few months. And don't forget to give your treating doctor your full medical history before sitting for a session. Botox is extremely versatile and can be used to:

1. Relax frown lines.
2. Reduce crow's feet.
3. Relax forehead lines.
4. Reshape the jawline (for example, to soften square-shaped faces).
5. Provide relief to sufferers of hyperhidrosis: Botox can reduce excessive sweating in the underarms, hands or feet.
6. Lift or bring down the eyebrows.
7. Remove or lessen a 'gummy smile'.
8. Lift sagging jowls.
9. Reshape the nose non-surgically.
10. Reduce platysmal bands or neck lines.
11. Improve the drooping of a mouth, that is, make a 'sad mouth' into a 'happy mouth'.
12. Increase the length of the chin.
13. Help alleviate migraines.

New uses are being found for Botox all the time, which we will discuss more in Emergence. And it's a myth that once you start using Botox, you need to keep using it. It is a non-surgical, reversible treatment and when you don't update the procedure, it reverses.

SLOW-TOX

So how do we apply the 'less is more' principle with injectibles?

It's simple. Say I'm injecting a client with Botox. Now, as we know, Botox relaxes the muscle it is injected into. Overuse and therefore over-relaxation of the muscle can make the client's face look expressionless until the effect of the Botox begins to wears off. To avoid this, instead of injecting her or him with a six-month dosage at one shot, for example, I divide the dosage and administer half of it first, wait for three months and administer the other half – same dosage, but spread out over a longer time frame. As Botox is charged by the unit, the clients not only pay only for what they use each time but also enjoy far more natural results. You want to look warm and expressive, not cold and emotionless. No One Has To Know.

IV. THE GUIDE TO DERMAL FILLERS

If Botox is a relaxant, a dermal filler is a volumizer. As we age – if you remember the chapter on the Ageing Continuum – we lose fat on our face from areas like the cheeks as the fat pads migrate downwards, leading to hollows on the face and the face starting to look 'sunken'. Fillers plump up the lines and hollows left behind by lost fat and collagen. At the moment, the most popular filler is hyaluronic acid, a complex sugar found naturally in many tissues. Hyaluronic acid fillers are more expensive than collagen fillers but last longer.

Like Botox, fillers are reversible and need to be updated from time to time. But the exciting new thing to note is that where fillers were earlier just used to treat the nasolabial folds that is, the lines that extend from the nose to the mouth, and marionette lines that is, the lines that extend downwards from the corners of the mouth to the chin, the use of dermal fillers has exploded. They can also be used for:

1. Smoothening skin texture.
2. Adding contour to the sunken areas of the face.
3. Enhancing the shape of the face.
4. Removing fine lines.
5. Youthening the tear trough. With age, the 'tear trough' – that is, the area between the eyes and the nose – starts to look hollow as the fat pads start going south – and this makes the face look tired. Soft fillers can fill up and plump up the area.
6. Plumping up the cheeks. When it comes to fat pad migration, nowhere is the ageing process more apparent than in the cheek area. Reinstating volume into this area has an anti-ageing effect that few other cosmetic procedures can have.
7. Smoothening out the bridge of the nose. We go into greater detail about this in the chapter Excise.
8. Plumping up the lips. Using fillers to plump up the lips can be done at any age with beautiful results,

but the procedure needs to be done with care. Fillers can also correct thin, crinkled or inverted lips.

9. Tightening the neck. Even though you may take care, the neck and the back of your hands are a dead giveaway of your age. Fillers can lift sagging skin and obliterate superficial wrinkles in the neck, hand and décolleté area. This can be done in conjunction with skin tightening procedures.

Dermal fillers are incredibly sought after and work best when combined with other treatments like Botox and skin tightening.

When to use these tools and how to use them depends on the expertise of your physician. You may not even need any of it. If creases are only apparent when you squint or are animated, Botox is needed. If creases are visible at rest, and not made worse by squinting, then what you need are fillers. If creases are present at rest and get worse with facial expressions, then you need *both* Botox *and* fillers. In my experience, combination treatments always work beautifully. You relax the muscle with Botox, you fill with fillers, you tighten with skin tighteners. It all comes together.

But now comes the tricky part. A lot of the success of these procedures depends on the way they are done. There are bad Botox jobs and there are good Botox jobs. There are bad filler jobs and there are good filler jobs.

Let me put in the way that I understood it best. One of my friends sent over some kheer. It was thick, luscious and creamy and it was the best – to this day – the *best* kheer I have ever had. For the life of me, I couldn't figure out why it tasted so good. I dipped my finger in it repeatedly but, try as I might, I could not get it. Accepting defeat, I called up my friend. As it turned out, the mystery ingredient was a particular proportion of nutmeg. Nutmeg is not new to kheer but the way my friend used it changed my view of it forever.

All Botox and fillers are born equal. It's what you do with it. It's like the nutmeg. A pinch there, a pinch here. Dump a lot of nutmeg and that's all you will taste. Done delicately, it makes subtle and sophisticated changes, which you can't put your finger on. Doctors must be *extremely* sparing with injectibles. I would even advocate using far fewer units, stepping back, seeing the results and *then* booking the next appointment.

Because injectibles are meant to be your mystery ingredient.

That's what makes them so powerful.

Did you know that there exists a close connection between what you eat, your bowel movements and sagging skin? Did you know that the kind of food you eat could put your body in a state of chronic inflammation causing fine lines? Did you know that certain chemicals in food speed up ageing, bring on wrinkles and cause loss of skin elasticity? The fourth E, Eat, elaborates on how something as relatively simple as eating right can slow down ageing both on the outside and the inside.

The Fourth 'E'. Eat.
Because you are only as young as you Eat.

Food can age you. So many things you eat, depending on how it gets digested by your body, can prevent or hamper the supply of essential nutrients to the skin and other organs, ageing you both from within and without. And it's not just about the calories or whether you lose or gain weight. Depending on what you eat, food can tire you and nutritionally deprive you. It can also energize you. And cure you. Never underestimate the impact of what you eat and drink on how you look and feel. Food has the power to transform. Food has the power to heal.

In Eat, I've collated wisdom from the best experts around the world to help you identify food that ages you. As food habits are also some of the hardest to change, I'm also going to suggest small and medium-term changes so that you do not feel overwhelmed by trying to achieve too much in too short a time. It's worth the effort, though. Because the answers to your fine lines and wrinkles may just lie in the humble spinach leaf and because an unassuming *nimbu* may just save your skin *and* your body.

Because you are only as young as you eat.

FOOD THAT CONSTIPATES YOU AGES YOU

What's the connection between skin and your happy time in the loo? Well, if food is not getting processed through your digestive tract effectively, it could be the reason behind those fine lines and sagging cheeks. When the gut slows down and you are constipated, that's more waste sitting there in your intestine. And the longer the waste sits there, the more toxins accumulate. This, combined with stress, medications and irregular eating, compromises the efficiency of the liver, thereby affecting your skin and other organs, *ageing you*.

Secondly, when you're constipated on a regular basis, your body does not absorb nutrients, vitamins and minerals leading to malnourishment of skin, nails, hair and muscles. When the skin isn't well fed, it shows you up in fine lines, loss of tone and sagging. And I'm not even talking about the impact it has on the immune system, which could lead to infections and disorders and a general feeling of being unwell.

In this particular game of thrones, it is essential that you choose winning foods that make it to the finish line as efficiently as possible. Though it depends on your individual constitution, here are some foods that are likely to constipate many of you:[8]

1. Foods containing refined flour
2. Fried foods
3. Cookies and refined carbohydrates like cakes
4. Dairy products
5. Coffee
6. Chocolate
7. High protein diets: Weight-loss diets that skew in favour of protein can constipate, especially if the intake of non-vegetarian foods dramatically increases
8. Diuretics can lead to dehydration and can cause constipation

[8] '7 Foods to Avoid for Constipation Relief', accessed 30 December 2014, http://www.everydayhealth.com/constipation-pictures/foods-to-avoid-for-constipation-relief.aspx.

On the other hand, foods that *help* with constipation include:

1. Foods with fibre (roughage)
2. Banana, whole fruit (not fruit juices, though)
3. Papaya
4. Apricots, dates
5. Figs – fresh as well as dry

FOOD THAT INFLAMES YOUR BODY AGES YOU

Do you remember the last time you had a small cut? Or a small splinter that got into your finger? Pain would immediately shoot out and the area around the cut would go red. That is your body's natural inflammatory response to the foreign object piercing your skin. This inflammatory response, in turn, triggers the immune system to sending out white blood cells to heal the area that has been affected. The work that these cells do is two-fold: they repair tissue at the inflamed area and then switch off the inflammatory response, that is, the redness and pain slowly start to reduce.

Certain foods, however, keep your body in an inflamed state. What happens is that they falsely trigger the immune system to send white blood cells out to neutralize a threat that isn't actually there. With no cut or injury to heal, these immunity cells start floating aimlessly around throughout the body triggering cellular and molecular changes,[9] which not only are harmful for the body, but also affect your skin causing fine lines, ageing you. Studies have also revealed that a persistent state of inflammation can cause

[9] Elizabeth Peyton-Jones, *Eat Yourself Young* (London: Quadrille, 2011).

wrinkles and muscle loss as well as other diseases. Some foods that can inflame you are:[10]

1. Foods with additives, which would include many packaged and processed foods
2. Sugar: to include mithai, chocolates, doughnuts, sweeteners in yogurt and even tea
3. Dairy products
4. Peanuts
5. Foods with refined flour to include certain kinds of pasta, breads, pizzas, cakes and the like
6. Deep fried foods
7. Alcohol

It is not to say that all of these *cannot* be had in *reasonable* quantities; excess and continued consumption of these is what inflames your system.

FOOD THAT CAUSES OXIDATIVE STRESS AGES YOU

Oxygen is the giver of life. It's why we exist. On its own, it nurtures and sustains us but in the company of other molecules, it can destroy our health and well-being. Oxygen is a highly reactive element and – in a process called oxidation – reacts with other molecules it finds in food, in articles made of silver, in make-up or anything else it can react with anywhere in the world. You can see evidence of oxidation when a banana slowly starts to go black when left uneaten out in the open, or when the make-up you are wearing starts to look stale after a while.

[10] '6 Inflammation-Causing Foods No One Talks About', accessed 30 December 2014, http://wellandgood.com/2013/11/04/6-inflammation-causing-foods-no-one-talks-about/.

In the same way that fruit exposed to air begins to go bad, the process of oxidation also happens *within* your body and if not checked, can rot your insides.

And here's how: oxidation creates free radicals, which are 'unstable atoms with an unpaired electron'.[11] As free radicals look for electrons to complete the pair, they steal them from other atoms within proteins, genes and other healthy cells – including skin cells – located in other organs of the body. This, in turn, leads to the creation of more free radicals as the atoms they steal the free radical from now become unstable themselves – as they also now have an unpaired electron – leading to a destructive domino effect. This is what is called oxidative stress. Free radicals have a pretty bad reputation: they been linked with diseases ranging from the common cold to diabetes to arthritis to cancer. They have also been linked with dents in collagen bands, which result in the formation of deep lines or wrinkles, ageing you.

So what triggers the release of these bad boys? Free radical levels can be raised via eating the wrong foods like foods high in fat as well as foods high in chemicals, but also via pollution, smoking, stress, weight gain, recreational drugs or even too much sun. Our bodies naturally fight free radicals with their own antioxidants. But there comes a time when too much is too much and there's only so much a body can fight back on its own.

Since we know that free radical triggers include excessive sun exposure, smoking and so forth, it makes sense to

[11] Elizabeth Peyton-Jones, *Eat Yourself Young.*

bring about lifestyle changes by cutting back in areas, which you think are toxic for your health. But, of course, not all lifestyle changes are feasible; for example, what if you are a beach entrepreneur running a watersports shack in sunny Goa? That's where diet comes in. You'd therefore be saving your skin, and possibly your life, by consuming food designed to eliminate free radicals: antioxidants.

Antioxidants are Vitamins A, C and E and minerals like selenium, manganese and magnesium. They are also carotenoids like lycopene and lutein and polyphenols like flavonoids and resveratrol. How antioxidants work is that they 'neutralize free radicals by giving up an electron to bond with them'.[12] Foods that contain these are also called free radical scavengers. So while you may not be able to eliminate free radicals entirely, you know what to do to reduce them significantly. And you can start by eating the next paragraph.

Coloured fruits and vegetables like berries, mango, papaya, carrots, pumpkin, tomato, spinach, broccoli, lemon, sweet potato, beet and wheatgrass are rich in antioxidants. I also advise my clients to drink as much vegetable juice as possible: you can just blend veggies in a juicer and drink. Antioxidant capsules work well too.

Some foods that trigger the spread of free radicals include:

1. Foods with chemicals, which include many packaged and processed foods and those with artificial colouring

---

[12] Ibid.

2. Foods high in fat
3. High GI (Glycaemic Index) foods[13] like refined flour, white rice, white bread and surprisingly fruits like melons and pineapple, chikoo, mango, custard apple and grapes

FOOD THAT UPSETS YOUR HORMONAL BALANCE AGES YOU

The delicate balance of hormones within our body is responsible for many wonderful things that include how good our skin and hair is, how well we manage our weight and how young we look. Among the hormones more relevant for the purposes of this book, I'm specifically talking about insulin, adrenaline, cortisol and, of course, the thyroid hormones.

To look young and to delay the onset of premature ageing, you need to take care of your insulin levels, keep the stress hormones, adrenaline and cortisol, in check and also maintain your thyroid hormones, which dictate how you metabolize food. The delicate and interconnected balance of these hormones is deeply affected by what you eat, especially by the heavy consumption of fats, carbohydrates and sugars.

For example, foods high in sugar trigger an overproduction of insulin and an overload of insulin causes the skin to sag, facilitating the production of cellulite and triggering diabetes. Excessive lack or excessive production

---

[13] 'Combating Oxidative Stress: Healthy From the Inside Out', accessed 30 December 2014, http://www.nutritionvictoria.com/content/combating-oxidative-stress-healthy-inside-out.

of any particular hormone upsets the balance of the other hormones. And when your hormones are out of control, you start to put on weight, your skin starts to age and you start to look older than you are.

Some foods that upset your hormonal balance are:

1. Foods high in sugar
2. Foods high in fat
3. Processed foods[14]

FOOD THAT UPSETS YOUR ACID-ALKALINE BALANCE AGES YOU

It was my husband's diagnosis of terminal cancer that really drew my attention to the acid-alkaline balance of our bodies. A very dear friend of mine insisted on giving me a jar of something that was believed to have completely reversed the advanced-stage breast cancer of her friend's mother. Before she dropped it off, I was envisioning this high-tech bottle with complex compounds listed on the label. When I actually saw what she brought me, there was no label and it was barely a bottle; it was a small unassuming container of amber liquid – not even 50 ml – that cost a whopping 15,000 rupees. *This* reversed advanced-stage cancer? I thought to myself.

But, by now, I had heard of the doctor who was selling it and, frankly, I was ready to try absolutely anything to alleviate my husband's suffering. Before giving it to him, I tried a tiny drop of it myself. It tasted like honey with a little bit of soda but I didn't pay too much attention to it. At

---

[14] 'Common Causes of Hormonal Imbalance', accessed on 30 December 2014, http://www.mamashealth.com/hormonalhealth/hormonal.asp.

about the same time, recipes were coming in from all over for my husband. One such recipe included adding baking powder to maple syrup (without sugar) when the syrup reached a particular temperature. And then suddenly it hit me: these recipes for cancer patients were all trying to *alkalize* the system.

What we eat either has an acidic effect on our body or alkaline. The body needs to be more alkaline than acidic for us to feel and look both young and healthy. The more you alkalize your system, the more you prevent the further spread of diseases like cancer and the greater your ability to combat ageing.

It all started making sense: why wheatgrass shots are given to cancer patients, why so many of my doctor friends gave us liquid chlorophyll or soda bicarb. The chlorophyll, the wheatgrass, the soda bicarb, all this was helping to alkalize the system. Then I started thinking: What if we do this *before* the disease and the premature ageing have a chance to invade our bodies?

Acidity or alkalinity is measured on the pH scale (pH or potential of Hydrogen measures the concentration of the Hydrogen ion) from 1 to 14. A pH of less than 7 means that your body is more acidic. A pH greater than 7 means your body is more alkaline. If you score 7.1 to 7.4 on the pH scale, you are exactly where your body needs you to be: more alkaline than acidic. This range is perfect because you are neither too alkaline nor too acidic. At this level, your body is brimming with antioxidants, anti-ageing phytonutrients, essential minerals and vitamins, all of which will keep you young and healthy.

So how do you check if your system is more alkaline or acidic?
pH levels of the body's fluids and tissues can be tested using pH strips (given at the back of this book). Detach a strip from the booklet and dip it in your saliva or urine first thing in the morning before eating or drinking. Wait until it changes colour and then compare it against the colour guide on the booklet.

You are on track to combating ageing if the pH of your urine lies at about 6 in the morning and at about 7 in the evening. Similarly, if your saliva is at a level of about 7 all day, you're good to glow. I recommend that you test your pH one hour before or two hours after a meal.

So how do you make your system more alkaline?
Eat and drink your way to alkalinity. Diet has a potent effect on the body's acid-alkaline equilibrium. A diet which is about 60 per cent alkaline and 40 per cent acidic works to maintain the balance.[15] However, if your pH test depicts high acidity, the balance can be restored with the help of a diet that is about 80 per cent alkaline.[16] These are broad estimates, but you get the point. Keep testing your pH levels from time to time to keep track of the changes in your body.

Western diets are notoriously more acidic in nature as they include coffee, tea, meat, wheat, sugar, dairy, pastries, pizzas, pastas, cakes, bread and other foods that have refined flour as their base. All of these are acid-producing. Chinese food is pretty acidic as well. As a nation, we are

[15] Elizabeth Peyton-Jones, *Eat Yourself Young*.
[16] Ibid.

also slowly being inducted into the acidic hall of fame, as we are increasingly more influenced by Western fast food diets.

So which foods are more alkaline? Well, that's easy. Alkaline foods are also antioxidants. So anything from the list of antioxidants given earlier in this chapter will work to alkalize your system as well. I can also tell you the two things I do to maintain my alkaline levels.

First, I start my day with lime shots. When I first started guiding my Miss India girls twenty years ago, the dietician for the pageant used to give the contestants lime shots in the morning before they exercised. I used to wonder why but I never asked because we never had the time. But this practice kept coming back to me from different sources and I finally understood why. Lime is alkalizing. Though it's ironically acidic to the taste, it gets assimilated as alkaline in the tissues. The same holds true for other citrus fruits. *The innocuous nimbu is a master alkalizer.*

Second, I never step out of the house without my glass of green juice: it's spinach and water mixed in a blender and seasoned to taste. I tank up on antioxidant-rich, chlorophyll-rich spinach everyday. It's my green drink. And I urge my clients to do as I do.

Some foods that upset your acid-alkaline balance are:
1. Caffeine
2. Meats
3. Sugar and processed baked goods
4. Refined flour

ACID-ALKALINE BALANCE THROUGH THE AGES

The acid-alkaline balance is not a new concept. It was ancient practice to brush the teeth with a stick from the neem tree, also called *datoon*. This datoon stick was anti-bacterial and not only served the purpose of maintaining oral hygiene but also worked to cleanse the gut. Post cleaning their teeth, people would rinse their mouths to spit out or expel yellow fluid called 'pith' or bile – which signified an acidic system – and would continue to do so until the yellow changed to nearly white, showing signs of a clear gut, thereby maintaining the acid-alkaline balance the old-school way.

Without knowing why, babies are given gripe water for colic, fruit salt is consumed after a heavy meal, women who have recurrent UTIs (Urinary Tract Infection) have sachets of citrus soda with them, all indicating that we have been fighting acidity for decades, perhaps centuries, with alkalizing tools to make us feel better.

WHAT'S ON THE MENU?

At a glance, it doesn't look good. Most of the foods to avoid that are listed in this chapter taste oh-so-good but seem to be oh-so-bad. But the key here is moderating your intake; take the middle road if taking the high road is difficult to do. The inevitable next step – dietary changes – are some of the hardest changes to make and I really hope my baby-step approach helps you to ease into the process. Small to big, here are some of the smartest anti-ageing steps you can take.

Now
You can start this NOW

The Daily Lemon Shot

Choose four healthy medium-sized limes, squeeze them and drink the juice immediately. Do not add water. Avoid contact with your teeth and throw it straight to the back of your mouth. This should be taken on an empty stomach first thing in the morning or, alternatively, after a heavy meal.

The Daily Liquid Chlorophyll Alkalizing Smoothie

Take a bunch of coriander or broccoli or spinach or anything that is green and put about a glass of water in a blender. Blend it and strain it. Drink immediately because the moment you let it wait for more than two minutes, it is exposed to the air and gets oxidized thereby becoming dead juice with no nutritive value.

Now
You can reduce this NOW

Sugar

Sugar is one of the most ageing foods that exist and an overload of refined sugars or foods containing sugar (pastries, cakes, sweet beverages and the like) trigger disease and ageing. Before buying or ordering, study food labels extremely carefully. Sugar isn't always listed as sugar: it can manifest itself in various forms like fructose, dextrose, high fructose corn syrup or anything ending in -*ose* like glucose, sucrose and more. And that's just one avatar of this deadly ingredient. Do a little research before you step into a supermarket the next time. Even sugar substitutes need to be dodged. Like the plague.

Salt

An overload of salt is also incredibly unhealthy and ageing. And the worst part is that it creeps up in packaged goods, processed foods and in so many other products that you would never think would have salt in them. Again, read your labels. Try to choose foods lowest in sodium. Unless otherwise specified by your doctor, 3 grams of salt per day is enough.

Later

Increase 'colour' in your diet over the next few months. Deeply coloured, vibrant food products, fruits and vegetables have been known to give a tremendous boost to antioxidant activity as compared to other foods.

In the Long Term
Make simple changes over time

1. Eat grilled or boiled or steamed or baked food instead of the deep-fried variety.
2. Go easy on dairy. Milk is acid-forming, so it needs to be offset with alkalizing foods such as vegetables.
3. Go easy on meat, especially processed meat and red meat.
4. Ditch bad fats like transfats, hydrogenated fats and saturated fats, and eat good fats like monounsaturated fats, omega-3 fats and omega-6 fats in the appropriate quantities. These kinds of fats are present in some nuts

like walnuts and almonds, fish and oils like corn oil, sunflower oil. Olive oil is also good for you.

5. Avoid processed and packaged foods and foods high in preservatives and additives.

The best thing about making dietary changes is that they start showing results in a comparatively short amount of time. There's nothing indicated in any of the above pages that won't do wonders for your health in general. A little adjustment here, a little moderation there and you can steadily notice how the bloating, weight and puffiness goes down and your youthful energy goes up. You will look and feel younger, fresher, faster. With the increase in life expectancy due to advancement in modern medicine, we have been granted *quantity* of life. But what's quantity without *quality*? Food for thought.

Did you know that exercise is one of the most powerful anti-ageing tools? Did you know that your skin is so forgiving that even if you start NOW, you can begin to look younger faster? Did you know that there are certain workouts for your face that speed up – and beautifully complement – the anti-ageing process? The last of the 5Es, Exercise, is designed to help you understand what a beautiful thing exercise can be. Both for your skin and for the rest of you.

The Last 'E'. Exercise.
Because you are only as young as you Exercise.

What I'm about to tell you is bad for my business.

To understand the role of exercise as an anti-ageing tool is to first understand the role of *blood* as an anti-ageing tool. Blood is your body's 'delivery boy', carrying with it 'food' to various parts of your body in the form of nutrients and fresh oxygen. Fresh blood also brings with it the ability to wipe out toxins and free radicals from the area it is flowing into. The part of the body receiving that will therefore be 'flushed' clean.

Skin, like all the other organs, needs to be fed and flushed for it to best perform its functions that include looking supple, glowing, bright, tight and *young*. Exercise ensures that fresh blood – with all its nutrient goodness, fresh oxygen and toxin-fighting ability – reaches your skin. It is one of the most underrated anti-ageing tools there are.

If you're reading this chapter up until this point, my guess is that you're pretty unimpressed. In fact, you're probably just short of rolling your eyes at this. You have heard this before; it has been said. Yet, you still don't do it. But why? Could it be that while you understand the concept, you may not really understand its importance? Maybe it's like the statutory warning sign on cigarette packets; after it has been repeated so many times, the warning loses its value. But that is a pity because I will go as far and say that I could perhaps lose half my business if my clients just made it a point to exercise with greater frequency, wear sunscreen and eat the right food.

I was treating a thirty-three-year-old client for PCOS-induced acne when she was preparing for running her first half-marathon. At every consult, she would update me on her progress. She used to talk about the members in her group and who among them impressed her with their speed or were the ones to watch out for. She had always assumed that the people she was running with were in their late thirties and early forties. But on the day of the race, when she saw them in their full running gear, complete with running bibs – the number which all marathon runners have to pin on themselves– she couldn't believe what she was seeing: the people she had been training with all this while now had the words 'veteran' and 'senior veteran' on their bibs. Which meant that, contrary to her presumption, some of them were in their early to mid-*fifties*. She was mystified. I, on the other hand, was not.

What made the runners look at least ten years younger? Could it be that they *all* had fabulous genes? We don't know that; it would seem like too much of a coincidence. But we do know for sure that they had one thing in common: Exercise.

WRITTEN IN BLOOD

The blood delivery system in the body is intricate and beautiful. Fresh blood is pumped by the heart into the aorta, our largest artery. From the aorta, blood then flows into other arteries as thick as our little finger and further into thinner and thinner channels like the arterioles and finally into the thin, hair-like capillaries. The further the blood has to travel from the heart, the thinner the channels for its distribution get. It is these thin capillaries – as thin as a strand of hair – that finally supply blood to the skin.

The skin is the last organ to receive fresh blood; the last to receive fresh oxygen and nutrients.

As we get older, the channels supplying blood within our body start to get blocked. Bigger arteries start to get obstructed. I'm sure we all know someone who has got an angioplasty done to open up these blockages: a friend, a relative, a parent. The point I'm trying to make is that if the thicker arteries, as thick as our little finger, could get blocked over time (upto 99-100% blockages sometimes), then what about the tiny hair-like capillaries supplying blood to our skin? Isn't it possible for the tiny channels to get blocked *far sooner*? They could have been blocked in our teens. And the longer the capillaries are blocked, the longer our skin has been without fresh blood, the duller and *older* we look.

So what, then, does exercise do? *Exercise forces fresh blood to surge through the capillaries and reach the skin.* Raising your heart rate – especially through cardiovascular exercise – pushes blood through blockages or resistance in your capillaries thereby reaching the skin. If your heart beats, say, seventy-eight times a minute, fresh blood is pumped that many times a minute. But if the exercise you do increases your heart rate to say about 110-120 beats a minute,[17] blood is pumped faster and more furiously, supplying nutrients and fresh oxygen and cleaning up toxins and free radicals. Which is why when you emerge from a game of squash or a running session, you look flushed and more pink, shining and fresh. Which could be

---

[17] This will vary depending on your age, health profile and medical advice from your physician.

why, after doing this for years, marathon runners looked about ten years younger.

Depending on the exercise you do, the effects on your skin could last up to 24-48 hours post the session. So, for your skin, exercising 4-5 times a week is enough. Exercise as per your age, fitness ability and health profile. If you're sixty-five, you can sign up for the same training programme as a thirty-five-year-old, but only if it has been okayed by your doctor. If you're suffering from heart ailments, high-intensity cardio is perhaps not the best option for you. My brother-in-law is pushing sixty and skips 500 times a day. If I tried the same thing with my bad knee, I pretty much may as well give up on getting out of bed altogether.

Apart from cardio, you could do yoga; it gives you a good workout. Strength training with weights boosts your heart rate, improves your bone mass and helps prevent osteoporosis, especially for women around the time of menopause. Do what suits you, your lifestyle, your budget. You can never go wrong with a brisk walk about 4–5 times a week.[18]

You can also incorporate exercise into your daily life. Wear or carry a pedometer, which counts the number of steps you take in a day. Increase your amount of daily activity. Park your car at some distance from your destination and walk the rest of the way. Walk short distances to the grocery store. 10,000 steps a day is effective not only for the skin but also for weight loss. Anything works, so long as it's done with regularity.

---

[18] Before starting any physical exercise, check with your physician.

FACING UP TO EXERCISE

Exercise is one of the most potent anti-ageing tools there are. But we've only spoken about exercise for the body. What about exercises for the *face*? The face and neck are made up of over fifty muscles and if we can tone the muscles of our body and have them looking leaner, stronger, fitter and more toned, then why can't we do the same for the face? Skin is elastic and has its own resilience and as the muscles become stronger with exercise, so does the skin, its outer covering.

One thing to note about exercising the muscles on your face, though. Many of these small, superficial facial muscles are inserted *into* the skin. So when the underlying muscle is exercised, there is a chance that the overlying skin can get dented or crinkled due to excess movement. Which is why the facial exercises prescribed in this chapter are only for the 'levator' muscles, the big muscles of the face and neck.

The following exercises for your face and neck are a perfect add-on to anti-ageing treatments but not a substitute for them. Before trying these, however, make sure you get a go-ahead from your physician in case you have spondylitis, vertigo or other ailments that would require you to take care while exercising your head and neck; facial exercises should never be a pain-in-the-neck. You can choose your exercise depending on the areas or area you want to target or even choose them all but don't overdo them as you can fatigue the muscles of your face. These exercises are designed to be done anytime and anywhere: in the shower, behind the wheel at a traffic signal or behind your boss's back.

Forehead

THE FROWN DROWN

FOR THE FOREHEAD. HELPS REDUCE FROWN LINES AND
FOREHEAD LINES.[19]

1. Sit down in front of a mirror
2. Put your elbows on the table and gently prop up your forehead with your fingertips. Keep your head upright and look straight ahead.
3. Now, gently push your fingers up towards the hairline. Hold this position against your bone.
4. Without moving your head and still looking straight ahead, gently attempt to bring your brow down against the pull of your hold, while slowly closing your eyes.
5. Maintain this position for a count of three. You can repeat this three times about thrice a week.
6. This exercise is non-obtrusive and can really be done in any situation.

[19] Eva Fraser, *Feel Fifteen Years Younger with Eva Fraser's Face and Body Programme* (London: Penguin, 1993).

Eyes

THE DESK SQUEEZE

FOR THE AREA AROUND THE EYES. HELPS REDUCE PUFFINESS.

Desk jobs tire the eyes, make them sluggish and reduce circulation around the eye area. Again, this exercise is as simple as it is non-obtrusive, which means you can do it without your colleagues noticing and putting your antics in the next month's newsletter. This particular exercise works to improve the circulation in your eyes and also improve muscle tone, all good news for anti-ageing.

1. Look away from your laptop/screen.
2. Focus on something a little farther away. It could be anything – a colour, a pattern, an object.
3. Squeeze the eyes shut for five seconds.
4. Repeat this three times taking a break of thirty seconds each time.
5. You could do this daily.

Cheeks

THE SNEAKY CHEEKY

HELPS GIVE THE ILLUSION OF HIGH CHEEKBONES.

1. Sit in front of a mirror.
2. Gently clench your back teeth, but do not apply pressure. Keep your lips apart slightly.
3. Give a small smile so that your *upper lip* moves upwards. This will lift the muscles of your cheeks upwards,

matching position #1 on the diagram. Hold this position for five counts.

4. From this position, now give a 'medium' smile, wider than the last smile but not your widest smile. This will lift the muscles of your cheeks further upwards and will match position #2 on the diagram. Again, hold for five counts.

5. Now, give your widest smile, which will lift your cheeks to the highest position #3. Again, hold for five seconds.

6. In three slow movements, come back down. From your widest smile, go back to your 'medium' smile or position #2 and hold for five seconds. Now, go back to position #1 – small smile – and hold again for five seconds. Return slowly to the starting position.

7. Breathe and relax for thirty seconds. Repeat steps 3-6 above for the next set.

8. Do a total of three sets three times a week with breaks of thirty seconds between sets. And try not to squint or squeeze your eye muscles. It works best if you can keep your eyes wide open.

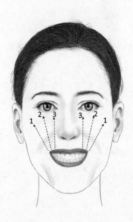

THE UPPER CHEEKY

FOR THE UPPER CHEEKS.[20]

1. Wear cotton gloves or take a tissue in each hand because this exercise requires you to put your thumbs in your mouth. You can also do without them, but don't tell me I didn't warn you.

2. Sit in front of a mirror, with elbows resting on the table.

3. Silently pronounce the letter 'O'. Keep your mouth in the 'O' position.

4. Now place your thumbs inside each side of your mouth between your back teeth and your cheeks. The nails of your thumb should be facing your teeth inside your mouth and also pointing towards the top of your ears. This may sound complicated but once your thumbs are inside your mouth, you'll know what I mean.

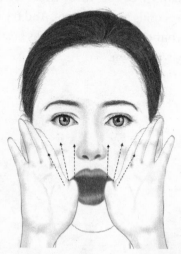

---

[20] Ibid.

5. Your palms should be facing outwards, towards the mirror.
6. Move your thumbs upwards. You will feel your mouth stretching wide open as your upper cheek muscles move upwards. Keep trying to maintain the 'O' position.
7. Hold for a count of five.
8. Bring your mouth back to the starting position of 'O'.
9. Relax and breathe. Repeat thrice with breaks of thirty seconds between sets.
10. You can do this three times a week.

THE LOWER CHEEKY

FOR THE LOWER CHEEKS.[21]

1. Repeat Steps 1 to 3 from the previous exercise.
2. Now, when you place your thumbs inside each side of your mouth between your back teeth and your cheeks, ensure that while the nails of your thumb are facing your teeth inside your mouth (like the previous exercise), they should also point towards the *middle* part of your ears.
3. Again, your palms should be facing outwards, towards the mirror, same as in the previous exercise.
4. Now move your thumbs *outwards towards the angle of the mouth*. You will feel your mouth stretching wide open as your lower cheek muscles move outwards. Keep trying to maintain the 'O' position.
5. Hold for a count of five.
6. Bring your mouth back to the starting position of 'O'.

[21] Ibid.

7. Relax and breathe. Repeat thrice with breaks of thirty seconds between sets.
8. You can do this about three times a week.

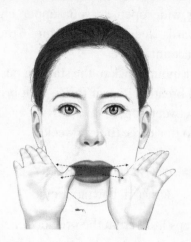

THE FISH FACE

QUICK LOWER CHEEK WORKOUT[22]

1. Sit or stand in front of a mirror.
2. Breathe in, breathe out two or three times.
3. Jut your chin out.
4. Now do a fish face (like we used to do as kids),and suck in your cheeks for about ten counts.
5. Release and relax. Breathe in and out a few times. Repeat steps 3 and 4.
6. The Fish Face should be done three times in a row with breaks of thirty seconds between sets. You can perform this exercise thrice a week.

[22] Ibid.

Chin

THE CHIN PRESS

FOR THE CHIN AND FOR DOUBLE CHINS. OR FOR AS MANY
CHINS AS YOU MAY HAVE.

1. Drop your head backwards, stretching as far as you can
   comfortably hold it in that position. Take a deep breath
   and hold for a count of five.
2. Slowly releasing your breath, bring your head back up
   to starting position.
3. Take a deep breath and turn your neck towards the left
   till you feel a pull in the muscles of your neck. Hold
   again for a count of five.
4. Slowly releasing your breath, bring your head back to
   starting position.
5. And, finally, take a deep breath and turn your neck
   towards the right till you feel a pull in the muscles of
   your neck. Hold for a count of five.

6. Slowly releasing your breath, bring your head back to starting position.

Do a repetition of three sets for this exercise three times a week for the double chin and neck. Don't forget to take thirty-second breaks between sets.

Neck

THE JOKER[23]

YOU HAVE TO GRIN AND BEAR THIS FACIAL EXERCISE, WHICH REQUIRES YOU TO OPEN AND CLOSE YOUR MOUTH IN A WIDE SMILING POSITION. THIS SMILING ASSASSIN WORKS TO SLAY THE LINES AROUND YOUR NECK FOR TIGHTER NECK SKIN AND A MORE CHISELLED JAWLINE.

1. Stand or sit down in front of a mirror. Keep your back straight.
2. Now slightly tilt both your head and your back upwards. Just slightly, though.
3. Stick your chin out.
4. Keeping your head still, lower your jaw. This will open up your mouth. The next step is to grin as widely as you can.
5. At this point, try and close your mouth, keeping your face in the 'grinning' position. Feel the tightness in the muscles around your lower jaw and neck.
6. Now, still grinning, relax and breathe once.
7. Still grinning, open and close your mouth ten times, focusing on lowering and raising your jaw.

[23] Ibid.

8. Do three sets (it is ten times per set) three times a week. Take a thirty-second break between sets, though.

Don't forget to maintain the wide grin position throughout. During the exercise your focus should be on lifting and lowering the jaw. Also, do not clench your teeth and take care to ensure that there is no tension either on the forehead or the area around the eye.

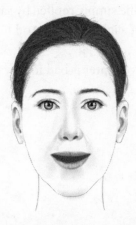

Like I said, you can choose the exercises as per the area you wish to target. And if there are multiple exercises that target the same area, you can choose any one you like. However, more is always merrier.

A friend of mine was suffering from trigeminal neuralgia, a neuropathic condition affecting the trigeminal nerve resulting in intense pain in the face. Finally, she addressed the condition with the help of gamma knife treatment. While her pain subsided, the facial muscles on one side of her face weakened, leading to asymmetry.

But she didn't want to go in for a facelift or fillers without trying the alternative routes first. She had a different plan. Which consisted mostly of facial exercises.

Day or night, she never missed her date with her face workouts. I didn't see much difference initially but when I met her after a gap of a few months, her face was symmetrical again; it was like nothing had gone wrong. The first thing I asked her was if she had had any work done to her face. She simply replied by saying that she was fanatic about her facial exercises. And here I thought she had fillers done.

Like I said, this chapter is bad for my business.

4

H
H
A
I
R

While not a part of skincare, hair is one of
the most age-defining parts of your body.
The Only 'H'. Hair.

In the 1800s or early 1900s, television was not an entertainment option. The travelling circus, then, with its gigantic, glorious tents, trapeze artists and exotic animals may have held infinite fascination for the young and old alike, not to mention its eagerly awaited special acts. Parents of that generation would probably have paid good money just so that their children could see this:

The Bearded Lady

One of the more notable features of the circus acts of yore, the Bearded Lady, was often the subject of mockery, contempt, or even simpler, naked curiosity. People would queue up in lines as she quietly revealed herself to gasps and squeaks alike. Whether it was money well spent or fodder for nightmares for years to come, she never failed to disappoint.

The erstwhile pheno-menon of the Bearded Lady, like many similar erstwhile phenomena, has a simpler – and unfortunately not as exotic – explanation now. If you are female and growing a beard, you don't have to spend your life in a circus tent. It's a hormonal imbalance, either hirsutism, hypertrichosis or something similar that's behind this particular growth spurt. It can be completely cured, which

means that people won't be paying money to see it. Now you simply pay money to remove it. Unless, of course, you *want* to keep it. Then this part of the book may not be for you.

Hair presents a curious paradox. In so many cases, it simply never grows where you'd like it to or recedes where you'd want it to. Yet, this elemental feature of ageing contributes significantly to the way we feel about ourselves and how old we look. This chapter will talk about both Hair Removal/Reduction and Hair Restoration.

Because sometimes we are only as young as our Hair.

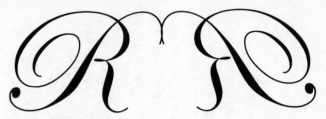

Removal/Reduction

Restoration

Laser treatments? Threading? Waxing? What are the best solutions to remove or reduce unwanted hair? Part I, Hair Removal/Reduction, will provide you with both temporary and long-term ways, to include:

a. Temporary hair removal
b. Long-lasting hair reduction
c. Hormone-induced facial hair reduction

Are you experiencing premature hair loss? Thinning? Alopecia? Part II, Hair Restoration, will outline the best solutions to get the hair back on your head and the spring back in your step. We'll cover:

a. Causes for hair loss
b. Solutions and cures

Hair Removal / Reduction

Whether it's the unibrow that's been annoying you or the hair on your chin that suddenly seems to have sprung up from nowhere, this table will feature the best forms of temporary hair removal and side-effects, if any. I'm not going to go into too much detail because most of this is known to you. I'm just listing them here so that you know how each compares with the other and you can make an informed choice.

A. TEMPORARY HAIR REMOVAL

Hair Removal Technique	The Science	Suitability and Side Effects	Regrowth
Plucking	Most of us are familiar with plucking, threading or tweezing, which is the mechanical technique of pulling the hair from the root.	Works for hair removal from smaller surface areas. While it's generally harmless, it may cause irritation and ingrown hairs.	This method of hair removal, though temporary, is thorough as hair is pulled from the root. Plucked hair takes longer to regrow than methods such as shaving. Safe for anyone over the age of sixteen.
Threading	With the help of a twisted cotton thread to pull hair from the root, threading removes short lines of hair at a time.	Good for short lines of hair, mainly for facial hair. Again, it's generally harmless but an inexperienced technician can cause the hair to break causing faster regrowth, or there could be minor cuts if the thread pinches delicate skin.	Depending on how your body works, hair regrowth takes about two weeks. Again, this is safe for anyone over the age of sixteen.

Hair Removal Technique	The Science	Suitability and Side Effects	Regrowth
Waxing	Warm wax is applied to larger surface areas of the body like legs and arms and the hair is pulled out at the root from the opposite direction.	Almost any part of the body can be waxed to include the legs, bikini area, arms, abdomen and feet. However, I do not recommend waxing facial hair like the upper lip and eyebrows as it irritates the skin often leading to rash and pimples. I would also not advise waxing the chest or the back as it triggers acne breakouts. Waxing could also lead to ingrown hair.	Hair comes back in about 3-4 weeks. Suitable for those sixteen and over.
Shaving	Using a hair razor, this technique slices hair on the surface of the skin.	For women, shaving body hair is a good alternative to waxing it. And it doesn't spell doom for your hair regrowth. That's a myth. Hair quality or regrowth is not affected by shaving. In fact, I would	Because the hair is cut on the surface of the skin's, regrowth is, needless to say, faster than waxing.

Hair Removal Technique	The Science	Suitability and Side Effects	Regrowth
		recommend shaving over waxing for areas with thicker hair growth like the pubic region and underarms.	
Epilators	Epilation uses an electrical device with a rotating head consisting of either small tweezers or a coiled spring/wire, which is used to trap the hair and pull it out from the root.	Never use epilators on delicate facial skin. Strictly not recommended for facial hair.	Epilators can be used for anyone above the age of sixteen.

Hair Removal Technique	The Science	Suitability and Side Effects	Regrowth
Depilatory Creams	Depilatory creams have active ingredients that weaken and break hair bonds so that it can be easily scraped off the surface of the skin.	In order to break the hair bonds, it needs to be left on the skin's surface for some time. Leaving such a strong cream on the skin for long periods is not recommended, at least not by me, but you can use depilatory creams if you can't seem to book a waxing appointment or your razor or epilator has gone missing. Strictly not recommended for facial hair.	Like shaving, the hair is removed from the skin surface or just below skin level. Hair regrowth is therefore relatively quicker than waxing. Can be used for anyone above the age of sixteen.

WILL THE HAIR GROW THICKER AFTER SHAVING?

This is probably one of the most popular myths there is and the

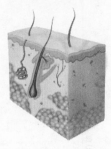 short answer is *no*. Whether you wax or shave, the quality of hair growing back remains unchanged even though it *feels* different. To understand why is to take a look at the image. As you can see, the hair shaft is thick at the bottom and tapers at the end so that the tip is the thinnest section of the hair shaft.

When you wax your hair, it is pulled out at the root, which results in the hair follicle temporarily becoming empty. When it starts to grow back, the thin tip is what first emerges, which is why waxing regrowth seems softer.

But when you shave your hair, it is cut at the surface of the skin at its widest part. Hair starts to grow from the point it is cut off, which is the middle of the hair shaft and also the thickest part of the hair. Which is why it feels so coarse growing back.

Shaving has zero impact on the thickness of the hair. Hair thickness depends on genetics and hormonal imbalances. Even the apparent darkening of the shaved hair is nothing but an illusion — it only appears darker because the little dots of hair are showing up against your skin. In fact, when done regularly, *shaving body hair can work better than waxing* especially on the legs, as it reduces ingrown hair and dark spots.

INGROWTH

When the hair curls up and grows back 'in' the skin instead of coming 'out' of it, that's when you know that you have ingrown hair. This could happen for many reasons: for example, if the hair is thicker than the diameter of the opening (follicle) or when two or more strands emerge from one follicle or even when hair is waxed or tweezed incorrectly and has not been pulled out properly. Hair can also grow inwards when dead skin and sebum and so on clog the follicles.

What works to reduce the incidence of ingrown hair is shaving, electrolysis and laser hair reduction. If you're not opting for laser, then alternate between shaving and waxing: every time you shave that particular area, wax it the next time. Additionally, exfoliating that area regularly will prevent the clogging of pores, reducing ingrowths.

But what if you want a more long-lasting solution?

B. LONG-LASTING HAIR REDUCTION

LASER HAIR REDUCTION

Lasers are attracted to the dark pigment or melanin present in the hair shaft. In turn, melanin absorbs the laser light and heat is generated, which causes long term or permanent damage to the hair follicle. The thicker the hair, the more melanin it has. The darker the hair, the more melanin it has. Which is why lasers don't work very well on extremely light or grey hair or very fine hair, which has little or no melanin. Light skin and dark hair is the *best* combination for this kind of treatment. The more melanin the hair has, the better the results.

Depending on how well it works with your body and the amount of melanin your hair shaft has, you may be able to reduce the hair permanently or at the very least, have *much* thinner hair growth than before. The new hair growing in could also be lighter in colour, which makes it less apparent, markedly extending your time between waxing or shaving.

Three Dos and Don'ts of Laser Hair Reduction

DO Keep a Gap Between Laser Sessions

Lasers target follicles with actively growing hair. Hair is always in different phases of growth and only some are active at a particular time. Depending on the individual and body part targeted, a gap of at least four weeks is recommended between treatments in order for a large group of follicles to become active and sensitive to laser treatment.

DON'T Wax or Thread Hair While Doing Laser Sessions

Waxing, epilating, plucking or threading yanks hair out from the root. This has the resultant effect of causing collateral circulation, thereby *reactivating* a dying hair follicle. Needless to say, this makes the laser session completely ineffective. Between sessions, shaving is therefore recommended.

DO Avoid Lasers After Getting a Tan

Tanned skin is darker and more sensitive. Since laser treatments target melanin, the first thing that will be targeted is the melanin in the tanned skin, which may lead to burns. As the laser treatment also involves heat, it may burn skin that is already tanned. Reschedule the appointment until after the tan has worn off.

As a final note, IPL (Intense Pulsed Light), though not a laser device, is also used for hair reduction. Other laser devices include the diode laser, ND Yag, Alexandrite, Ruby lasers, all of which differ based on their wavelengths. Your practitioner will be able to guide you.

ELECTROLYSIS

Electrolysis uses electric currents to destroy the root of the hair, after which the hair is manually pulled out with the help of tweezers. Though this method is more or less obsolete, it is brilliant at addressing long-term removal of grey hair. Electrolysis is the only thing that works for my older clients with excess facial hair, since lasers can't target their grey hair.

In unqualified or untrained hands though, electrolysis could lead to pigmentation and scars. Look for a qualified electrologist.

C. HORMONE-INDUCED FACIAL HAIR REDUCTION

Ashima Roy came to me with a full beard. Newly married, it was her husband's joke about sharing a shaving brush that got her to book an appointment with me. Shaving this kind of hair would help her keep it under control but she would have to do it every other day. Her facial hair was so thick that it could not even be bleached.

For women, the presence of excess hair on the face or its sudden appearance on other male areas of hair distribution is called hirsutism. The causes could range from genetic predisposition to Polycystic Ovarian Syndrome (PCOS) to overproduction of testosterone to, in some cases, even a side effect of medication. If you're a woman and have hair suddenly growing in unwanted parts on your face and body to include the midline below the umbilicus (the navel), the lower back or around the nipple (areola) of your breast and/or if your hair is thicker and coarser than is expected in females, do get it checked by a qualified physician: it's an external sign of a definite internal problem. Whatever causes it, it is nothing to be ashamed or embarrassed about, I told Ashima. There is an explanation. And, with very few exceptions, there is always a cure.

The results of her blood investigations confirmed my suspicion that she had PCOS. She also had mildly raised prolactin levels, which is why she had such hard hair on the face. I split her treatment into two parts: attacking the hirsutism by treating her PCOS internally via medication as well as addressing the symptom of excess facial hair through laser hair reduction.

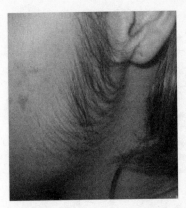
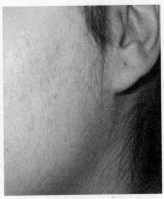

Laser Hair Reduction: Over time, in conjunction with various medications, lasers worked effectively to reduce this client's facial hair dramatically.

She had to be patient. It would take a minimum of 6-8 laser sessions with 4-week breaks in between to see satisfactory reduction in hair quality and quantity. It took time, but gradually, she saw the beautiful results and was extremely relieved. It was a close shave.

Hair Restoration

You're losing hair and you're losing your mind? Hair loss is as natural and inevitable to the ageing process as sagging necks and wrinkles are. Irregular lifestyle patterns, high stress, genetics and hormonal imbalances are all guilty of triggering early onset of balding or thinning hair.

Hair Loss

GENETIC	MECHANICAL	HORMONAL	INFECTIONS	DEFICIENCIES	AUTOIMMUNE DISORDERS	MEDICATION
	pulling of hair or tight hair styles	puberty	systemic diseases	haemoglobin	alopecia	chemo-therapy
		PCOS or other hormonal imbalances	severe infections	TSH		hyper vitaminosis (Vit A)
		pregnancy	surgery	protein		certain other medications
		lactation	fungal (local) infections	certain vitamins and minerals		
		peri-menopause				
		menopause				

Hair loss is not just a man's problem and is more common in women than you think. For every five men with hereditary hair loss, there are three women with the same condition. Hair loss can begin as early as in your twenties and by thirty-five, in many cases, almost 40 per cent of women demonstrate some of the symptoms. By fifty, half of all women experience some degree of hair thinning. It's enough to pull your hair out.

In the table given below are listed common reasons for hair loss with information about what you can do about it.

A. CAUSES OF HAIR LOSS

GENETICS

1 One of the most common – and also the most irreversible – reasons for hair loss and premature balding is genetics, passed down from either your mother's or father's side of the family. The more bald people you are related to, the greater your chances of losing hair. Unfortunately, it's a myth that balding skips a generation. It does not. Statistically, about half the people with a balding parent on either side of the family will inherit the dominant gene for baldness.

MECHANICAL

2 Traction alopecia – bald patches caused due to pulling of hair – occurs either when the hair is tied back too tightly or there has been consistent and routine pulling of the hair due to a hair-pulling disorder called trichotillomania. This condition manifests itself in the receding of the hairline or in the asymmetric loss of hair with broken hair across the patch. Multivitamins, topical applications and, in some cases, psychological counselling help cases of traction alopecia.

HORMONAL

3 Hair loss due to hormonal reasons could range from pregnancy to PCOS to menopause and even to the discontinuation of the oral contraceptive pill. To find out if you have PCOS, you need to test for LH, FSH and DHEAS as well as check your testosterone, androstenedione and prolactin levels. You also have to do a pelvic ultrasound. Depending on what your results are, hormonal treatments include spironolactone, a combination of ethinyl estradiol and cyproterone pills, among other lines of treatment.

INFECTIONS

4 Typhoid, severe infection and major surgeries can trigger hair fall. Localized infections like fungal infections or seborrheic dermatitis could additionally also lead to localized hair fall, that is, scaling of skin or thinning of hair. Surprisingly, hair fall is also part of the recovery process post cosmetic surgery, especially after a face lift or a brow lift as both these procedures mandate stitches in the hair follicles, causing hair fall. But this kind of hairfall is mostly temporary and regrowth occurs in about 3-4 months.

DEFICIENCIES

5 Iron and protein deficiencies could cause hair loss. Even crash dieting could temporarily do that due to dietary deficiencies. Supplementary vitamin pills, however, cannot prevent the hairloss that is associated with losing weight rapidly. Which is not to say that eating right doesn't reverse hair loss. That's why Eat is a separate chapter in this book and an integral part of my 5E Approach.

AUTOIMMUNE DISORDERS

6 Autoimmune disorders can also cause hair to shed. Alopecia areata is an autoimmune disorder and shows itself up as small round patches of hair loss usually seen on the scalp and beard. This is mostly reversible.

STRESS

7 Though not mentioned in the table on hair loss, during tough times, stress shuts down the body's ability to produce hair, since hair is not necessary for survival. In this mode, the body redirects its energy to repair vital body structures and so there is an increase in hairfall.

MEDICATION

8 Medication-induced hair loss includes that due to chemotherapy and other medicines like an excess of Vitamin A – a condition called Hypervitaminosis – as well as certain antibiotics, anti-fungal medications, anti-hypertensive medications, hormone replacement therapies, among others.

B. SOLUTIONS AND CURES

All is not lost. The first thing to do when you are losing more hair than usual is to rule out hair loss caused by reversible conditions. Hair loss brought on by stress or nutritional inadequacy or hormonal changes or even medication can be sorted out by eating right, dealing with your stress, taking the right medication or eliminating the offending one. While your medical practitioner will advise you about the way forward for most hair-related problems, take a look at some popular solutions for hair loss:

MEDICAL SOLUTIONS

While you need to check these with your doctor before starting them, there is something that you must know before reading further: you are born with a certain number of hair follicles. I repeat: *you are born with a certain number of hair follicles*. They cannot be increased but they can be reduced. Any treatment, practitioner or product that suggests that you can increase the number of hair follicles is, unfortunately, just plain *wrong*.

Minoxidil

Minoxidil is the only medicine for female pattern hair loss – which is usually the thinning of the hair on the crown, widening of the centre hair parting or a receding hairline – that has been approved by the Food and Drug Administration of the US. It was approved for men in 1988 and for women in 1991. How Minoxidil works is that it increases the blood flow to the scalp, which in turn boosts hair growth; 2-5 per cent Minoxidil topically applied aids in the microcirculation of the hair follicle, thereby helping hair growth. It usually works better for women than men. However, the downside is that it has to be continuously applied to sustain hair growth.

Finasteride

Finasteride was approved by the FDA in 1997 for male pattern hair loss – which presents itself as a receding

---

SNOWFLAKES IN JULY

Snowflakes in July? When dandruff starts to announce itself on your shoulders, collars and everything else, and when people can identify where you had been sitting by the powdery parting gift you leave behind, it's time to shake the flake.

Dandruff can be caused by one or many reasons. In adolescence, the scalp's sebaceous glands are more active, causing it to flake. And while many attribute dandruff to dry skin or loss of moisture on the scalp, true dandruff is due to an excess of oils, dead skin cells, pollution, sweat and dirt.

Does oiling work to cure dandruff? Well, yes and no. If your dandruff is due to overactive sebaceous glands, oiling won't help, because oiling will block pores and prevent moisture from entering your scalp, further drying it out and causing more dandruff. But oiling can work if the reason you're flaking out is because your scalp is dry.

If you can't figure out why you have it, there's no need to scratch your head. Get your doctor to help you with a correct diagnosis – especially if you have a chronic case – because medical conditions like psoriasis and seborrheic dermatitis can also cause this condition.

hairline in an M-shape or thinning of the hair on the crown of the head or in the form of a 'U', where hair remains just above the ears and at the back of the head. It is taken orally and works to preserve existing hair. It works by blocking the conversion of testosterone (the male hormone) into DHT (Dihydrotestosterone), which converts hair follicles into non-hair follicles, leading to hair loss. Finasteride can cause abnormalities in the growth and development of a foetus, which is why it is not usually recommended for women of childbearing age. It's pretty effective, though. Finasteride 1 per cent used under medical supervision have men reporting 30 per cent improvement.

COSMETIC SOLUTIONS

Hair-Building Fibres

Hair in a bottle can be a genie in a bottle for many cases of hair loss, especially when it is irreversible or genetic. Available both in spray form as well as in powder form, tiny fibres beautifully camouflage empty bald patches and thinned out hairlines. While the effect is temporary and usually has to be reapplied every time the hair is washed, I have seen some pretty realistic results.

Hair Weaving

Hair weaving tacks on matching hair to the original strand of hair via a tight 'braid' and can be wonderfully executed. When the hair grows out, the braid becomes loose; retightening needs to happen every six weeks.

Hair Transplants

Hair transplants are incredibly popular and need good donor hair to be successfully executed. Donor hair is the existing hair on the patient's scalp, which will be removed from one area on the head and transplanted to a part that needs hair. Hair transplants can be done in one of two ways: Surgeons can either remove individual hair follicles from the donor area and transplant them onto the bald patch or they can remove an entire strip of hair-bearing scalp, divide it into smaller grafts of one or a few follicles and then place the grafts onto the area being treated.

As with many other medical conditions, the best time to treat hair loss is always as early as possible as it responds better to treatment if caught early. After finding the cause, treatment should be complemented by vitamins and protein boosters in the form of supplements, iron, antioxidants and amino acids. Treatment should also be complemented by cheer, positivity, faith and self-love.

GENERAL HAIR CARE

To maintain her long, lustrous and still beautiful hair, Poonam Dhillon does simple things: she eats nourishing food, and takes care of her hair with oil and deep moisturizing, on occasion.

When it comes to taking care of your hair in general, I thought I could give you a few more bits of simple advice that have helped both my clients and myself over the years. *Less is more* works here too, and unless you have specific problems – like extreme dryness or oiliness – you don't need to go crazy taking care of your hair:

1. Condition the hair after washing and use a good anti-dandruff shampoo once a week.
2. Oil is best used as a conditioner. Despite many beliefs to the contrary, oiling doesn't boost the length or quantity of the hair but does do wonders for its *quality*. To condition the hair, beat 1 tsp of honey with 2 tbsps of olive oil and apply on the hair, especially on the lower ends. Wrap your hair in a hot towel for about thirty minutes. Rinse hair thoroughly with lukewarm water and towel dry; this serves to make hair really lustrous and you can do this once a fortnight or whenever you feel you need it.
3. Leaving oil in your hair overnight really doesn't do anything for it. Just use it to condition.
4. Take care of your hair by not subjecting it to frequent heat treatments like blow drying and ironing or chemical treatments and perming.
5. If you sweat a lot or feel your hair needs a wash often in a week, don't be afraid of washing your hair frequently. Just choose a frequent-wash shampoo.
6. And lastly, don't forget to cut or trim your hair regularly. It's the simple things that sometimes work the best.

5

The Small es of Skincare

This is the last set of Es that you will see in this book. These are the four small **e**s which, unlike the 5Es, are mostly *not* a part of my main, recommended skincare routine. What these small chapters will do, however, is address the remaining relevant questions spinning around in the world of skincare and, in the case of the chapter *express*, will help you with some smart, quick tips.

emergence will address the hottest, cutting-edge and emerging trends in skincare and what to look out for in the future.

excise will address the limitations of non-surgical treatments.

expert will address the best ways to choose an expert to treat you including deciding whether you need one in the first place.

express will deal with quick skin tips and bridal skincare.

If you have any lingering questions, they may also be addressed in this part of the book. You never know. Stay with m**e**.

EMERGENCE

In hot pursuit

In classic fairy tales or disaster movies or any other standard story, there is a beginning, a middle and an end. Whether the story is boy meets girl, villian meets challenger or zombie meets lunch, there will always be a progression towards some sort of ending even if it is in the form of the guy who swoops in, saves the girl and rides off into the sun. My only hope is that they are both wearing sunscreen.

The story of the non-surgical beautification industry however has *no* ending. So long as the need to beautify exists, non-surgical treatments – like other related industries – will *always* be stories in development. New services and products will try to top the last blockbuster in an effort to deliver quality results with minimum pain, downtime or side effects. Some will grow to be classics, while others will sink without making a mark and making you wish the company had offered you a refund. Upfront.

The first small e, emergence, will outline some of the hottest stories of non-surgical treatments as they unfold so that you know what to look forward to. Many of these treatments are still in the research or testing stages, while some have been around but are just waiting for the right break. Non-surgical procedures make up nearly 75 per cent of the cosmetic industry and aggressive research for newer and better machines and even more minimally invasive techniques is – and always will be – going on. However, while the information in the ensuing pages is both state-of-the-art and exciting, it's best to adopt a wait-and-watch approach for any new treatment till it starts to hit mainstream markets or till practitioners feel confident about administering them. Because every story has its own twists and turns.

FROTOX[1]

It's Botox's cool new cousin. Known by its alternate name 'Frotox', Iovera is a cutting-edge treatment in the field of non-surgical anti-ageing which uses nitrous oxide to temporarily immobilize the nerves controlling certain facial muscles with the outcome of mitigating wrinkles and lines, the effects of which last for about four months.

Nitrous oxide – 'cold shots' – are injected into the temples to reduce the appearance of vertical and horizontal forehead lines. These shots provide the nerve with an acutely cold 'shock' which has the effect of putting the nerve into 'sleep mode' for about four months, thereby enabling the muscles to relax and the wrinkles to fade. The Iovera procedure uses a technique called

---

[1] 'Move Over, Botox! Toxin-Free Wrinkle-Busting Treatment Using the Power of COLD Launches in the UK', accessed 30 December 2014, http://www.dailymail.co.uk/femail/article-2317018/Move-Botox-Toxin-free-wrinkle-busting-treatment-using-power-COLD-launches-UK.html.

'cryoneuromodulation' and is touted as the alternative to Botox. Frotox clients have also been known to experience more pressure than pain when the procedure is being administered.

If you want to know what I think, I think that because it's so new, the outcome is not as easy to predict as for tried-and-tested Botox, and I also think that it needs to be supported by more trials, studies and research to verify its long-term effects before I would consider it to be a workable and safe alternative to Botox and administer it to my clients. Having said that, it's one procedure to watch out for and it'll be exciting to see how this big story unfolds.

BOTOX IN CREAMS

While I have already discussed its transformative effects earlier on, Botox is continuously evolving. It is already available in the international market in the form of creams and topical applications, which will give you the effects of Botox without the prick of a needle. While there are versions that claim to erase lines and wrinkles, they don't work too well because the size of the Botox molecule used in these creams is too big to penetrate the barrier that skin puts up. Efforts are on therefore to further reduce the size of the Botox molecule or alter it so that it can reach the targeted muscle and work *this* smaller molecule into gels, creams and topical medications.[2]

---

[2] Nick Lowe, *The Wrinkle Revolution*, revised edition (London: Kyle Cathie Limited, 2007).

DERMAL FILLERS

The use of dermal fillers has exploded today. Besides the regular and common indications for which fillers are used as mentioned in 'Erase', dermal fillers are also used to 'cushion' the ball of the feet or the heel so that those who wear high heels can do so with all the glory and none of the pain. New-age fillers are also coming preloaded with xylocaine, an anaesthetic, with the express purpose of making the procedure less painful.

I'm currently working on trials, which entail injecting fillers into the scalp. This has the dual effect of temporarily increasing height and also making a flat scalp look more rounded.

SKIN ASTROLOGY

Would you like to know when you will wrinkle? Or when your hair will start to go grey? All you have to do is take a DNA test, which can be done through your saliva. Skin astrology works to predict how you will age so that you can delay or prevent its onset. DNA testing via saliva is available in India.

STEM CELL THERAPY[3]

Stem Cell Therapy is being widely hailed as the next magnum opus that would help human bodies battle cardiovascular issues, arthritis, hypertension, inflammation and more. Stem Cell Facelifts are a hot new

[3] 'Stem Cell Facelift', accessed 30 December 2014, http://www.youthfulneck.com/stem-cell-face-lifts.php.

trend that don't require any surgery but at the same time can completely rejuvenate your face. The procedure involves a) transplanting adult stem cells and fat from another part of your body to your face followed by b) rejuvenating both the transplanted stem cells and the local stem cells within the face by using certain kinds of stem cell growth factors. This treatment has the wonderful effect of restoring the shape and youthfulness of the face, tightening the facial skin and also evening out patchy skin colour caused due to sun damage and natural ageing.

Stem cell facelift technology is currently nascent in India, with many companies – both Indian and international – promoting it in various forms.

FAT FREEZE

Can you imagine a future where fat would not melt but freeze away? In this cool new technique called Cryolipolysis, fat cells are broken down with the help of *cold*, not heat. The broken-down fat cells are then naturally eliminated by the body. ProShockIce uses this technology via a combination of a plate-like device as well as acoustic waves to not only break down the fat but also smoothen and tighten the skin. The recommended course of treatment is about four to six sessions.

Apart from ProShock Ice, there are other companies who now also use this technology – after receiving FDA clearance in 2010 – for this non-invasive fat layer reduction treatment. This procedure protects the outer cell membrane and as a result, there is no scar tissue formation post treatment. It also helps to bring about a

20 per cent reduction in bulges, so it is especially suitable for the abdomen, flanks, hips and thighs and has also been known to help cases of 'pseudo gynaecomastia' (male breast).

THREAD LIFTS

Thread lifts employ the usage of the PDO (Polydioxanone) thread, slowly stimulating collagen production until the thread itself is completely absorbed by the body. Thread lifts can be used to:

- correct sagging eyebrows in a procedure called a brow lift
- enhance the jawline or the jowls
- enhance the mid-face area
- correct the double chin

Thread lifts – which we are now doing at my clinics – work best in tandem with other non-surgical treatments like radio-frequency for skin firming, fillers or Botox. Using thread lifts as part of a combination treatment will postpone the need for a facelift. While the difference is immediately noticeable, this procedure takes about three months for optimum results, which will last for upto twenty-four months, when done at regular intervals as advised by your physician. Further new developments in the world of thread lifts include the use of cogged threads – which give near-surgical results without surgery – and cannula threads as well as the use of this procedure for the under-eye area.

GLUTATHIONE (ANTIOXIDANT)[4]

Also known as Gamma-Glutamylcysteinylglycine, or GSH, Glutathione is a protein molecule that is present in our body and supports the immune system. Found largely in the liver, it is regarded by medical experts as one of the body's most effective and important antioxidants and its first line of resistance against oxidative stress. As we already know, oxidative stress contributes to ageing and almost as if to confirm that, there is a direct link between increased ageing and the reduction of glutathione levels. As we get older, our glutathione levels start to fall, and we lose the ability to fight the impact of oxidation.

Intravenous delivery (that is, through a drip) of pharmaceutical grade Glutathione and Vitamin C will not only keep immunity high, keep free radicals at bay and delay ageing, but will also help brighten the skin.

SKIN CELL CULTURE

The Skin Cell Culture technique – which is now available in India –involves taking a tiny sample of healthy skin, culturing it and using it for grafting onto the damaged skin. In this method, skin cells will be grown in a culture and then grafted on the damaged area. This will especially work well for people with vitiligo, where melanin can be grown in a culture and be transplanted onto skin which has lost its pigment. I have seen good results in those cases where the patches are not too extensive or if they are on non mucosal areas, that is, lips and eyelids.

[4] Nick Lowe, *The Wrinkle Revolution.*

SKIN CELL INJECTIONS[5]

Cutting edge research on skin cell injections are ongoing. These injections will inject stem cell cultures of fibroplasts *into* the skin, which will help the skin regenerate collagen and elastin which will go a long way in reducing lines and firming up the skin. My clinics currently have the PRP (Platelet Rich Plasma) treatment where an activated Platelet Rich Plasma is injected into the treatment area to bring about cell repair. It's famously called the Vampire facelift.

HAIR CELL CULTURE

Advances made in hair cell culture techniques will see a whole new world of possibilities for hair transplants. Instead of donor hair, hair cells will be grown in culture and transplanted onto the scalp. It's in the trial stage in India. Meanwhile, hair from body area (especially the beard area) is being used as donor hair to be transplanted on the scalp.

THE EVOLUTION OF LASERS[6]

Exciting stories are developing in laser technology. For starters, lasers will be more effective in dealing with problems of stretch marks, amyloidosis, deeper and more stubborn pigmentation and acne. We Indians have a lot of dark patches on the back, arms and sometimes on the legs (Amyloidosis) and it is usually hereditary. While application of bleaching agents help in reducing the

[5] Ibid.
[6] Ibid.

darkness caused by melanin, the protein molecule still needs to be acted on, which will be brilliantly done if lasers come to the rescue.

Lasers in combination with radio frequency are now also being developed to remove white/grey hair as lasers currently can't catch hair without melanin. And lastly, exciting work is being done in the world of radiofrequency and long wavelength laser devices that will work to reduce acne by controlling excess activity by the skin's oil glands. This is especially relevant for those who are currently resistant to current and standard lines of treatment for acne.

SUNSCREENS

Even sunscreens are making hay while the sun shines. Sunscreens are now playing the double role of protection *and* repair as they are now coming loaded with antioxidants and Vitamin A with the combined effort of providing protection *and* rejuvenation. Sunscreens with antioxidants are now available in India.

Not all of the above treatments or equipment should be – or have to be – used in isolation. Combining machines with lotions or injectibles can give you far better and longer-lasting results. However, as with anything new, it's best to understand exactly how the active agents and ingredients combine to give you the best possible results and it's best to choose a practitioner who you think understands this well. You can combine some of the above-mentioned treatments – for example, neuromodulators like Botox with filling agents like collagen and hyaluronic acid – using the dual mechanisms of expansion/reflation and relaxation to deliver what you want much more effectively as well as increase the longevity of the results.

Not only ingredients, you can also combine equipment: for example, radiofrequency current for skin tightening with micro-needling for collagen repair. These two effective technologies work well together to deliver far more powerful skin tightening, scar healing and collagen regeneration. In non-surgical treatments, in most cases, two or three heads are always better than one.

That's all we know for now. But the story is far from being over because so long as we continue being an audience, so long as we continue to queue up to get these treatments, there will always be a story that is designed to work just for you.

E
X
C
I
S
E

What are the limitations of non-surgical treatments?
What is the way forward?
Excise is about cosmetic surgery, its pros and its woes.

She came to me with a problem I couldn't solve.

Shlokha Radia had just waved goodbye to her third son who was moving with his new wife to a new country. At sixty-six, she had spent a large part of the last ten years taking care of a husband who ultimately succumbed to cancer. Her waking reality was plagued with worries about the uncertainty of his condition, concern for the quality of his life and trying everything possible to delay the inevitable. Which she ultimately couldn't.

When she walked in for a consult a year after her husband's passing, it was almost as if the last ten years had added a further decade to her life. She looked about seventy-five. I want to focus on myself now, she said: what can you do for me? Her skin slackness was so advanced that the only thing I could have guaranteed were endless repeat visits right back to me. I can help you, I told her, by telling you that I *cannot* help you. If you really want to try everything you can, then a plastic surgeon would be your best bet. I had to turn her away. It was a problem I couldn't solve.

Excise is not a comment on the moralities of plastic surgery or about growing old gracefully or even about the aftermath of surgical beautification. I am simply trying to indicate the point at which non-surgical treatments cease to be of use. When I mean non-surgical, as I mentioned at the beginning of the 5Es, I'm referring to creams, lotions, facials, peels, cosmetology equipment like microdermabrasion wands and even injectibles like Botox. Non-surgical treatments can be done in a hygienic clinic, are minimally invasive or non-invasive with little or no downtime, and the results last for about 6-18 months. But this chapter will deal with cosmetic or plastic surgery which takes place in an operating theatre, where invasive intervention is made to make more long-lasting or permanent changes and when the procedures require anaesthesia, hospitalization, more downtime, sutures and the like. Surgical beautification, for many, is the final frontier.

When it comes to plastic surgery, to believe in it or not, is not the question I ask because that is a question clients have to ask *themselves*. I can only provide you with an informed opinion. Can plastic surgery do what non-surgical treatments can't? Yes. Do non-surgical procedures have their own uses and advantages? Yes. Is one better than the other? Depends on what you want to do. Non-surgical treatments uplift and enhance but those who go under the knife have their own standards of beautification and are willing to go through far more demanding procedures for a more permanent solution.

But it is not always about standards. Surgical or non-surgical, not every request should be honoured. Case in point, a young woman of nineteen, Rashi Singhania, came to me with a picture of a Hollywood A-list actress in her pocket and hope in her heart. She wanted to have cheekbones like her stunning airbrushed idol and wanted me to fill her cheeks in. She then wanted a nose job, followed by breast implants. She wasn't even looking to make a career in films or fashion, where these kinds of procedures – and pressures – are far more common.

Her single-minded obsession and unjustifiable unhappiness with herself made me uneasy – she was already a very attractive girl. What bothered me was that she didn't want to look like a better version of herself; she wanted to look like a better version of *someone else*. I didn't want to try to appease an unhealthy obsession that didn't look like it could ever be appeased. So, like Shlokha, I decided to turn her away. But for different reasons. It was a problem I *could* solve. But didn't want to.

As Indians, like I have said earlier, we don't age as quickly as those with Caucasian skin for example. Thanks to the very skin colour we try so desperately to brighten, our beautiful brown protects us from the ravages of early ageing far better than lighter skin tones. The darker our skin, the slower it ages. Typically, Indian skin doesn't have the problems of hanging jowls, overhanging neck skin or lines around the mouth that are common to Caucasian skin. But there comes a time when even the best non-surgical attempts to turn back the clock won't work. And at some point, even Botox, fillers, peels, microdermabrasion and the like will be helpless against the march of time.

WHAT NON-SURGICAL TREATMENTS *CANNOT* FIX

UNDER-EYE FAT BAGS

1 While non-surgical treatments can reduce the appearance of ageing under-eye fat bags – where these can be made to look less protruding – they can't remove them completely. There are two surgical methods of doing this. Clients can opt for the conjunctival approach where the under eye is everted (turned inside out) and a tiny cut is made, the fat pads are removed after which the incision is closed with an absorbable suture. The second method, the external approach, involves a cut in the natural crease close to the margin of the lower eyelid. Whether the procedure is external or conjunctival depends on the size and laxity of the skin under the eyes and is a call that is taken by the surgeon. The operating doctor then removes the fat pad, trims the excess skin and closes it up with tiny sutures in the eyelid margin. For women, a little bit of make-up – a simple kohl pencil – can further cover up the stitches but it is optional. As the suture line is close to the eyelid, the scar is barely noticeable.

ADVANCED AGEING

2 At the age of sixty-five and over, the sag in the neck or jowls is heavily advanced or the caving in, that is the fat pad loss, is so much that even if the client has a limitless budget for non-surgical treatments – which is usually not the case – and even by injecting fillers and Botox, tightening the skin with lasers, brightening and texturizing the skin as well as basically going crazy trying everything to help achieve a client's dream, I'd be lucky if I delivered even *half* of what he or she wanted.

Surgery works better in these cases. Amongst the thousands of cases that come to me with problems of advanced sagging skin, a mini surgical face lift will not only pull up the sagging skin and jowl, but will also tighten the double chin, jaw line and neck. The risks are that of any normal surgery but the results are longer lasting and will save the clients the six-monthly visits to me as well as the costs that come with it. Additionally, Upper Lid Blepharoplasty corrects drooping or hooded eyelids surgically and the sutures are hidden completely in the natural folds of the skin.

However, non-surgical procedures work well for the mouth by making it 'happy' instead of 'sad' (drooping down). In a combination of techniques, skin tightening procedures along with a few units of Botox as well as hyaluronic acid fillers have gently – but definitively – altered the face below. No surgery needed.

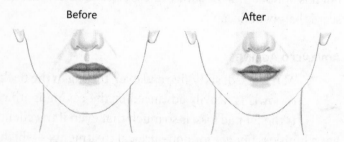

Before   After

EXCESS FAT

3   This one's a bit tricky. The thing with surgical intervention for excess fat is that the alternative

of healthy diet and exercise is always there, trying very hard to drown out your thoughts of liposuction. Diet and exercise is always the best and first line of action for excess fat loss with very few exceptions. And it's not just me. The surgeons operating on you will tell you that.

What I can do therefore is tell you this: liposuction works extremely well for fat removal but if you think you can wave a big fat goodbye to exercising and eating right, don't bother raising your hand. Any attempt at cutting fat through liposuction will fail if you don't follow through with post-operative adjustments to your lifestyle. If your heart is still set on it though, and all else being equal, fat loss through liposuction does *not* reverse if you exercise and eat right; it can be maintained for life.

The other point I want to make is that diet and exercise don't always rival liposuction. There are times when no matter how much sweat you leave behind on the treadmill or how carefully you eat, you still may not get the results you want. You may be excessively pear-shaped or, despite being underweight, you may just have two chins instead of one because it's a genetic gift you got. So if it is that important to you, liposuction may be the solution.

One of my clients, a very focused beauty queen, was determined to conquer both the ramp and the world. She was tall, had lovely features, but no matter how much she ate right and worked out, she couldn't get rid of the side fat on her thighs, which was hereditary; her saddle bags seemed to rule the ramp more than she did. She opted for liposuction, reached the top three at Miss India and won the Miss World pageant for us. In such cases where the person is focused, eating well, exercising well and it may be necessary for him or her to move up ahead, then sometimes liposuction may be the only viable option.

While we're still on the surgical removal of fat, I must mention that the tummy tuck or Abdominoplasty cuts out excess abdominal fat, flattening the abdomen. It's a good option for the formerly obese, when you've lost many kilos that could lead to loose skin or extra fat deposits around the stomach. Tummy tucks may also be a viable alternative for women who have had multiple pregnancies or multiple births (twins or triplets or more). The key thing to note here is to postpone a tummy tuck until *after* a pregnancy. Additionally, if you are indeed planning to lose a lot of weight, plan the surgery *after* you have achieved your weight loss goals; tummy tucks aren't designed to be an alternative to conventional weight loss methods.

And lastly, I can't conclude here without giving you information on bariatric surgery – surgery for weight loss. Bariatric surgery is for the clinically and morbidly obese and the guidelines for this kind of surgery are stringent. Not everyone with a weight problem actually qualifies for it so if you really feel you need it, check with your doctor if you tick the right boxes. And it's not the easy way out either. This kind of surgery has tremendously demanding post-operative requirements but may be the only light at the end of the tunnel for some.

LIPO-CRISIS?

If you've been swaying towards non-surgical fat removal, then you may want to read this. Lipolysis is designed to remove fat deposits in targeted regions of the body including double chins as well as fat around the waist, abdomen, under the upper arms, knees, ankles, inner thighs. It also promises to battle cellulite. If you'd like to know how it works, lipolysis uses fat-dissolving compounds like phosphatidyl choline, which is injected into the area you want to target (but should *never* be used on under eye fat pads). The procedure is performed usually by specially trained doctors and involves painless micro-injections. Theoretically, it also improves the body's fat-burning ability. And while we're still talking about the theory of things, in related information, the i-Lipo way of Lipolysis also conceptually works to eliminate and metabolize body fat.

I am not sure about these in practical implementation, though. We did similar procedures over five years ago when it was *the* thing but we stopped after seeing minimal results. The fat loss is temporary, even if the clients watch their diet and exercise, and while it does show inch loss, it would seem that the only thing my clients lost was water.

AUGMENTING BREASTS

Breast augmentation is not just sought after by models and actresses but now also by housewives and working professionals. Again, I can tell you about the pros and the woes and leave it up to you. Breast augmentation is like any other surgery: it comes with its own risks, that is, anaesthesia, how you take to the surgery and all other associated risks. Just choose your surgeon with care and don't go blindly by ads. Take your time.

What I would recommend though is moving only one cup size at a time, and not opting for too big an implant as what I've noticed is that those who go up two cup sizes usually tend to stoop after a while because ageing and menopause automatically increase the breast size. Smaller breast implants are better in the long run. Of the many plastic surgeries, breast augmentation is usually the most successful where clients are the happiest with their results and there isn't too much downtime either.

THE SHAPE OF THE NOSE

5 Non-surgical treatments can do wonders for the nose but can't completely reshape it. I'll tell you what I mean – say you walk into my clinic with a small hump on the nose that's been bothering you for a while. This can be fixed using fillers: I can put a filler above and below the hump, thereby filling both the hollows and straightening out the nose.

Non-surgical treatments also work well for clients who feel that their noses are too flat. Flatter noses can be raised and the width reduced with the help of fillers and Botox, thereby reducing the appearance of the 'flared' nostril, among other corrections. These kinds of treatments take minutes, are extremely effective but need to be repeated every 4-8 months.

However, for other kinds of nose reshaping, surgical procedures are the best option. A note of caution though: surgical nose jobs can be extremely complicated, especially when it comes to reshaping the nose. Sometimes, even in the most experienced hands, the desired correction can go a little off centre, so do take this step after some thought.

CHINS

6 If you go by the rules of facial aesthetics – as most cosmetologists have been taught – the face is divided into three parts and these parts must be proportionate to or about equal to each other for optimum facial aesthetics. The first part extends from the hairline to the middle of the eyebrows, the second part extends from the middle of the eyebrows to the tip of the nose and the third and last part is from the tip of the nose to the chin. Now, as per the rules, each of these three parts should be equally proportionate to each other. Indians – in most cases – have smaller chins, so the last part is typically smaller and not always in proportion. Going by these rules of facial aesthetics, if the person has a small chin, definition, shape and augmentation can be given with dermal fillers. But even in such cases, I especially recommend surgery to my clients for long-term results.

MOLES

7 Brown or black raised marks/growths on the body can be flattened non-surgically but the scar can sometimes present itself as a black mark. However, very deep moles or moles that are growing in size or become painful or start to bleed should only be removed surgically. For safety's sake, always insist on a biopsy after the procedure.

BALDING

8 Premature balding can be addressed with medicines and topical lotions, but a hair transplant is really the only effective long-term solution. Good donor hair for the transplant is essential. Donor hair is the existing hair on the patient's head that is transplanted from one part of the head to another and serves as the base for the new, transplanted hair. Having said that, trials are on in our clinics for regrowth of hair with a combination of Platelet Rich Plasma and peptides as an alternative to using donor hair.

FIXING BURNS OR PROSTHETICS OR THE AFTER-EFFECTS OF CANCER

9 Not all plastic surgery has been designed for aesthetics alone. In so many cases, plastic surgery provides a new lease of life to victims of acid attacks, mastectomies in breast cancer, burns, accidents, birth deformities like cleft palate, lipomas, facial palsy and other such conditions. Non-surgical treatments will have little or no impact in these cases.

There are a few exceptions, though.

Sitting with her parents huddled and worried in the waiting room, I could immediately see what Sameera's problem was. The left side of her face was drooping down, a deformity from birth. Her nose was leaning to the left side of her face and her left eyebrow and cheek were lower than the corresponding parts on the right side. It was like the left side hadn't caught up with the right. She was self-conscious about her appearance, unhappy and lacked confidence.

I first told her that this was a correction that only surgeons could do. But she didn't have the money for that. Keeping her budget in mind, I had to be smart with the tools I had. I corrected the left side of her face by adding volume to her left cheek, lifting her left eyebrow and using filler and Botox to widen her eye and straighten her nose. I reviewed her a week later and the results were amazing. She was as happy as I was. The next time I saw her was eight months later – the procedure needed to be repeated every 8-10 months –and she came with some news. She had found the confidence to put herself out there and came with a box of sweets to celebrate her engagement. Again, she was as happy as I was.

While the above addresses the most common surgical cosmetic procedures, there are many more available, and if it is something you need or want, you must have a conversation both with yourself and with a qualified doctor. The pricing for them – like all other surgeries – can range from a basic 'x' to possibly 100x, depending on the surgeon operating on you, where you're getting it done from and the kind of procedure you want. Doing your research before surgery is crucial and the choice of surgeon can make all the difference between doing it once and doing it again and again. And again.

And, just like with non-surgical procedures, 'less is more' works here too. Dr Daniel Baker – a pioneering plastic surgeon based in New York – has sculpted the faces of Madonna, Sharon Stone and other hot Hollywood A-listers. The thing that I love most about the way he

AVOID THE KELOID

If you do eventually elect to have surgery, and while most of it is safe, check if you have keloid tendencies. Keloids are formed during the healing process post-surgery. Instead of your body forming clean scars, keloids are scars that are bumpy and raised. Do inform the doctor during your consultation if you think you have this particular tendency or do ask him or her more information about it.

works is that he turns patients away if he feels they don't need surgical intervention and if he does work on them, his results are very natural. If this is something you want to do, try to choose a surgeon who you think can be honest with you.

BEFORE | AFTER
Do Non-Surgical Treatments Make You Look Worse After?

The question I'm often asked is that if I stop doing non-surgical procedures, will my look or skin deteriorate as compared to before I had the procedure? Well, the short answer is: No. You're so used to your face looking so much younger that when it starts coming back to its original form, you feel you look worse than when you started out. But actually, you don't.

I take 'before' pictures of my clients and when they look at them when the procedure starts to reverse, they notice that their muscles are *still* in a slight state of relaxation so it is better than before. So the answer is that it's never worse than before, it's always about 10 per cent better.

Many clients also try non-surgical options first as a dry run to surgical procedures; this way they can see how they might look post-surgery or can explain to the surgeon exactly what they want. And, as non-surgical procedures are reversible, if they do not like what they see, they can go back to the way they were.

These are mostly what surgical procedures can do for you. But, remember:

WHAT NON-SURGICAL TREATMENTS OR SURGERY CANNOT DO IS

Fix Your Life

You do cosmetic surgery because you want to enhance or transform the existing you according to the standard you have set for yourself. But if you expect plastic surgery or any kind of non-surgical treatment to fix your marriage, get more friends, make more money or simply be happier, then maybe you're better off actually trying to *consciously* fix your marriage, make friends, make money or be happier.

Then there's the darker side. Young men and women with possibly undiagnosed BDDs or Body Dysmorphic Disorders, where the young are crossing the limits and going in for life-altering surgical procedures. Young girls who have done their breasts, their nose and liposuction want more: lips plumper, legs thinner, waists smaller, feeding unrealistic obsessions.

Cosmetic surgery can be dangerously addictive. And so can non-surgical treatments. How can they it not be? Let's say you come to me to sort out your forehead lines. Once the look changes, you start looking at yourself in the mirror for more flaws. You notice that your cheekbones – which you have never noticed before – is spoiling the beauty of your face, or that's what you think. So you get that done. You scrutinize your face again. Are your eyes – which had never bothered you earlier either – looking too small? Hmmm. And that's the beginning of *no* end. The more you see your face, the more imperfections you notice and the more appointments you book. You're an adult. Know when to stop. Draw your own line.

Try and make peace with yourself before you decide to go in for surgery or excessive non-surgical procedures. That should be your first line of treatment for yourself. To enhance yourself but also know when it's not *you*. And, most importantly, to know the difference between loving and hating yourself.

What to look out for
when choosing an expert.

BIG PRINT. SMALL PRINT.

Finding an expert to take care of your skin and hair has never been so easy. Or so hard. With so many new beautification chains, experts and product lines being launched day after day, how do you choose what's right for you? In the third small e, expert, we will talk about what steps of caution you should take when you're choosing the right person to treat you.

BIG PRINT
New Clinic. Introductory Offers. Discounts. Discounts. Discounts.

SMALL PRINT
While starting a working relationship with a new clinic or
expert, try and find out their true face.
To save yours.

The relationship between your face and the people working on it is one of complete and absolute trust. When clients come to me to fix their skin problems, I know I am the caretaker of *the* most visible and definitive part of their entire body. It's a tremendous privilege and an immense responsibility.

Don't be too easy with your trust. See whether the expert you are choosing is truly qualified to do the job you want them to do, whether it is solving acne problems, using peels or injecting you with Botox. Look out for their qualifications on their website and their certifications on their wall.

Secondly, *experience* is the hallmark of a good skincare practitioner. I've been treating the skin for over twenty years, including fifteen years with injectibles, and I still have bad days at the office.

On the other hand, though, this becomes a chicken-and-egg story. If a practitioner doesn't get a chance to get experience, how will they *get experience*? True. There are many young and talented cosmetologists and doctors who do amazing work. My only advice to you is not to rush into any procedure. Set up an initial consulting session with the clinic or doctor: it's usually free or comes at a relatively nominal rate. Sit across the table and try and see if he or she is the best person to handle your problem.

Big Print
Have you tried our imported thermal laser zipper zapper?

Small Print
Make sure that they solve the problem you came for.

During this first consultation, see if there is *heart* in the counselling. Is the practitioner really listening to you, or is he or she recommending procedures you did not ask for? You'll be able to understand if they are in it for you or for the bottom line. If the doctor listens to your problems, is addressing the *primary* issues that are truly troubling you and is providing good, effective solutions, then you know that they are in it for the right reasons. To help you.

Everyone who gets skincare treatment comes to clinics or doctors for something that is bothering them: sagging jawline, crow's feet or acne. Make sure that what you came for has been acknowledged and is being addressed. About 70 per cent of the clients I personally consult come back to me to start the treatment. Because it is essential that a doctor shows genuine empathy.

BIG PRINT
DOESN'T OUR SHINY NEW CLINIC LOOK NICE IN THE PICTURES?

SMALL PRINT
How clean is the clinic, *really*? Hygiene is everything.

When you come in and sit in the waiting room for your initial consultation, see how clean the clinic is. No matter how nice it looks in the ads, inspection up close is vital. Are there scuff marks on the walls? Do the washrooms have a strong odour? Are they using gloves and disposables? Do you feel that dust has been sitting there for days? All else being equal, a hygienic clinic is best placed to deliver the best possible care for your skin. The last thing you want is to catch an infection from bacteria sitting on equipment that hasn't been cleaned properly after the previous appointment. Because that thing goes on your face.

BIG PRINT
YOU'LL BE WRINKLE-FREE IN 6 SESSIONS. FOR LIFE.

SMALL PRINT
How transparent is their promise?

Transparency is key to building a good relationship with your skincare practitioner. If a procedure needs downtime or further minor procedures or has side effects and needs antibiotics to counter them, it is the doctor's or cosmetologist's responsibility to let you know exactly how much time and expense it is going to take. Also, if a cream contains mild steroids or some other combination you may want to know about, the doctor *must* inform you. While the hallmark of a practitioner with integrity is someone who *volunteers* all this information, ask as many questions as you possibly can during your initial consulting session before you take a decision. Forget about the other people in the waiting room and take your time.

While choosing the best person for you, word-of-mouth is your best bet, better than full-colour ads or humongous billboards. If someone you know has had a good experience with a particular clinic, then be confident and go book your appointment. The chances of you getting disappointed are far fewer.

And very importantly, be cautious about those who

cannot keep a secret. While talking to you, is the doctor naming other clients or dropping names of their celeb A-listers *without* their permission? Chances are that they might name you in their next case study. Without you knowing or wanting it. At my clinic, we take client confidentiality *very* seriously. No one knows the number of stars and celebs that come to us but whom we have promised we will not name, even for this book.

WHEN DO YOU NEED AN EXPERT?

You don't always need to go to an expert.
It's best to go:

1. If there is a problem that persists beyond two weeks or more or is worsening.
2. If the condition is affecting your self-confidence, hampering your productivity and the way you feel about yourself.

Whatever you do, don't self-medicate.
If needed, at best, take an anti-allergy pill and
see your doctor at the earliest.

DOC, DOC.

WHO'S THERE?

When starting any new relationship with a cosmetologist or dermatologist, be fearless. Ask *lots* of questions. Don't worry about offending the doctor because it's your skin, your face, your life, your money. This short list is based on what my clients ask us and should make it easy for you to get the best of the resources available to you.

1. How long will the procedure take?
2. What kinds of products will be used?
3. Will it hurt?
4. What does the procedure entail?
5. When will you be able to go out in the sun?
6. Will anyone know you have done anything (if it matters to you)?
7. Will there be bruising or swelling or other post-procedural effects?
8. What are the other side effects?
9. What about when the effects wear off? How will you look then?
10. Has the doctor done this procedure on himself or herself?
11. Is the procedure popular with celebrities? (It's always a good sign if it is sought after by people in the glamour or beauty business.)
12. How soon will the results show?
13. How long will the results last?
14. Downtime: how much time will you need to take off? Will you have to miss work?
15. How much does it cost? Why is it so expensive? What kinds of components will the costs include? Are there hidden costs?
16. Lastly, ask if any of the drugs that will be used or prescribed have steroids in them. Steroids aren't always bad. For example, ointments with mild steroids may help with the severity of the condition and can be used for a short, prescribed time. But it's always good to know.

Non-surgical treatments are a two-way process. You need to help out someone who is giving you treatments because depending on what you get done, some are contraindicated for pregnancies, disease and other such similar exceptions. Depending on the procedure, your doctor or cosmetologist will need to know:

1. If you are pregnant. Or planning to get pregnant. If you are a woman reading this, it's the absolute *first* thing you need tell your doctor. Many procedures are contraindicated for pregnancy and even if you're *planning* a pregnancy, you need to inform your practitioner to prevent even the slightest risk to the baby.

The doctor must also know:

2. How much sun exposure you have had.
3. If you have undergone similar procedures in the past.
4. If you have undergone surgery recently.
5. If you are taking any medications, especially blood thinners.
6. If you have a pacemaker or any sort of metal implant in your body.
7. If you have recently recovered from a major illness.
8. If you have a history of keloid tendencies, which means that your skin does not heal normally after an injury or cut and the scar formed is hard and lumpy.
9. If you are using any topical creams at the time of treatment.
10. If you have any known allergies or recent infections.

11. If you have already had fillers injected, and what kind of fillers.
12. If you smoke.
13. If you're stressed at work or otherwise.
14. If you have a history of G6PD deficiency. G6PD is an enzyme that enables the normal functioning of red blood cells. Deficiency of this enzyme – which is an inherited condition – can cause anaemia, In these cases, certain groups of medication are contraindicated and cannot be prescribed.
15. Your expectation/outcome from the treatment and the time you have or expect to see the results in.

Answer all questions truthfully; I cannot emphasize enough how important it is for your doctor to be fully aware of your relevant medical history before injecting or treating you. A good, carefully chosen practitioner can delay or reverse ageing at any point in life. It's never too late to maintain a standard – any standard – that you have set for yourself if you believe that it is the best way for you.

The right help is out there.

And it is waiting for you.

Quick Skin Tips

Just because you've been bad doesn't mean you shouldn't look good. The last chapter of them all, express, will address quick fixes to common skin problems – including for those of you who have fallen off the skincare wagon – as well as some assorted wisdom that I have gleaned over the years that I just *had* to share with you. And, if you're a bride, this section will also give you the best way to prep yourself on your big day.

DARK CIRCLES OR PUFFY EYES

Out partying and slept too late or not for long?

1. Chill two slices of cucumber in the fridge and place one on each eye for about 10-15 minutes. It will reduce the puffiness.

   OR, chill two slices of raw potato in the fridge and place one on each eye for about 10-15 minutes.

   OR, dip two chilled pieces of cotton in rosewater and place one on each eye for 10-15 minutes.

2. You could also substitute the above with chilled, used tea bags. It works to reduce the puffiness and will also keep the skin around the eye hydrated. Caffeine constricts the blood vessels that contribute to the swelling of the eyes.

3. When done on a regular basis or every day, the above methods really work in mitigating the effect of dark circles.

4. Make-up also works beautifully to conceal evidence of a sleep-deprived night. Camouflage dark circles with concealers that have a yellow undertone, as the colour contributes to the natural look of our Indian skin better than pinker formulas.

UNDER-EYE FAT BAGS

The fat bags under your eyes – which is a natural part of the contour of your face as explained in The Ageing Continuum – can reposition themselves or swell up, because the area around the eyes has more spongy tissue. To help reduce this, sleep at a higher angle, which you can do by adding an extra pillow and sleeping on two pillows instead of one. You'll wake up looking less tired. You can also reduce your salt intake to further help reduce their appearance.

BAN THE TAN

Out in the sun and now feeling the heat? Reduce your tan with the help of this plan:

1. Buttermilk works like a charm. Apply chilled buttermilk on the tanned area and leave on for ten minutes. Wash off with cold water. Apply a soothing cream or lotion or calamine. You will see a visible reduction in the tan.

2. Mild bleaching two or three days after sun exposure helps eliminate the tan beautifully. However, if you

have sunburn, give a break of ten days before using bleach.

ALCOHOL-INDUCED DEHYDRATION AND PUFFINESS

If you have overdone the cocktails, alcohol-induced dehydration could show up the next day in the form of dull, dry and puffy skin. And, of course, a possible hangover. While I may not be able to help you with the hangover, I can definitely help you with the skin recovery.

1. Because alcohol is a dehydrating agent, the first and most important thing you can do for your skin the morning after is to re-hydrate. Drink lots of water with lime because your goal is to make your system as alkaline as possible and the lime helps with that. Just avoid caffeine as it could lead to further dehydration.

2. You can also apply a hydrating facemask for a few minutes. Alcohol dulls the skin; hydrating masks do well to reverse the damage.

3. Ice reduces swelling. If your face is puffy or swollen, fill a bowl of water, add lots of ice cubes and immerse your face in it. Sounds like medieval torture, but actually reduces the swelling significantly.

SUDDEN ACNE BREAKOUTS

What's that on your face? If you feel a pimple coming on, stop it in its tracks with these simple steps:

1. Take off all your make-up.
2. Cleanse your face well.
3. If the pimple is painful and shows a 'pus point', apply a dot of multani mitti or fuller's earth on the point

and leave it on overnight. It'll shrink the pimple beautifully.

On the other hand, if the pimple is painful and there is no pus, and if you're looking for an immediate solution – if you're getting married the next day, for example – I recommend going to your dermatologist for an intra lesional injection. The pimple will disappear overnight.

RASH

Feel a rash starting up? Make it go away by using calamine lotion to soothe the skin and taking an anti-allergy pill. However, if the rash persists or worsens after 24 hours, get it checked by your doctor. And, until things are back to normal, try to avoid rash decisions like applying make-up or trying out new skin products.

STAINED NAILS

While eating a fabulous Indian meal can touch the spot like little else can, eating with your hands can also leave your nails looking yellow. To sort out this problem:

1. Take half a lime and rub it on your nails. Do this for a few minutes.
2. If the stains are stubborn, though, put a little bleaching agent on your nails for about 3-4 minutes and wash off. Next, rub a little oil on the cuticles. Sure cure.

I'd also just like to point out here that if your nails look yellow without any particular reason, do get it checked out by your doctor. Yellowed nails could be a symptom of deficiency or disease.

DRY HANDS AND FEET

If you're suffering from dry hands and feet, remedies are simple and effective:

1. Rub coconut oil over the affected areas. Coconut oil is now available as a compressed compound, making it easier to both carry and use.

2. For dry feet, on waking up, soak your feet for thirty minutes in warm water which has 1 tsp of coconut oil and a few drops of shower gel. When your half hour is up, exfoliate your feet gently with a pumice stone. Alternatively, you could also apply an emollient to your feet at night, put cling film and then socks over them. You'll wake up to softer and suppler feet.

3. Lastly, if you are constantly using water for activities like washing vessels, clothes or anything else, choose prevention over cure. Use gloves before you subject your hands to water.

LONG-HAUL FLIGHTS

Due to cabin pressure and air conditioning, skin post a long flight can look drier, duller and older. Once, when I was on my way to London and even though I had moisturized my face before leaving, when I looked into the mirror after a few hours on the plane, I was shocked: I looked at least a decade older – and this was about fifteen years ago, when I had younger skin. I slapped on whatever moisturizer I could find and it served to reverse the dryness completely. After that, whenever I take long flights, I make sure that:

1. I moisturize my face every 2-3 hours.

2. I put lubricating drops in my eyes as and when they get dry
3. I drink plenty of water
4. I stretch and walk around as much as possible

Additionally, if possible, rub or massage a rich moisturizing cream – that suits your skin type – on your face for about ten minutes the next morning. Without wiping off the cream, put a hot or warm napkin on the face for two minutes, followed by applying a soothing mask on your face for about 10-15 minutes. You will also do well to hydrate yourself and catch up on your sleep.

DRY, FRIZZY HAIR

If hair that looked great the night before looks like birds have camped in it the next morning, you can tame the dryness or wild frizz – that could be brought on by mousse, hairspray or other hair products – by:

1. Washing your hair with shampoo and a detangling conditioner. Detangle while still wet, by running a wide-toothed comb through your hair.
2. If washing your hair is not possible, apply a leave-on conditioner and wrap your hair with a hot towel. Leave on for 20-30 minutes.

DRY OR RED EYES

For dry or red eyes:

1. Use non-medicated, lubricant eye drops 2-3 times a day.
2. Blink or scrunch the eyes. This will allow tears to flow easily into the eye, naturally lubricating it.

3. Avoid wearing contact lenses for a few days.

CHAPPED LIPS

Zip chapped lips by using a chapstick every hour and by refraining from biting or licking your lips.

BRIDAL SKINCARE TIPS

If you're about to get married or are planning the perfect wedding, say 'I Do' to the following recommended skincare regime:

- Start working on your skin as soon as possible. 3-6 months is ideal but the earlier the better, especially if you have problem skin. Do note that treatments like laser hair removal and acne scar resurfacing need to be done *months* in advance.

- As soon as your wedding date is fixed, get in touch with a dermatologist, gynaecologist and a cosmetic physician, if needed. Depending on the condition of your skin, treatment sometimes involves the inputs of all three specialists. Choose good, trusted people to handle your skin; if something goes wrong, you may not be able to fix it in a rush.

- A cleanup/facial is recommended once a month, depending on your skin type. If possible, take hydrating facials – they will nourish and moisturize your skin and add that much-needed glow.

- A full body bleach is advised once a month. When done well, bleaching eliminates tan, brightens skin and sloughs off dead skin.

- For hands and feet, invest in monthly manicures and pedicures. Gel or acrylic nail extensions also work, especially for the all-important close-ups of the ring.
- If you think you have an ageing lifestyle, change it. Drink lots of water. Eat well, eat balanced and eat at regular intervals. And even though you're rushing around, try to sleep on time and sleep well. Be a rested, happy, healthy bride: you will glow from the inside out.
- And lastly, do note that if you are planning to get pregnant soon after your wedding, please inform your doctor. As already mentioned, some skincare treatments and medications are contraindicated before and during pregnancies.

For both the bride and the bridegroom:

Do

- Have trials in advance for everything to include clothes, hair, make-up and shoes.
- Take care of body odour and bad breath, which can be sorted out in advance.
- Keep an emergency kit ready to tackle sudden outbreaks of rash or acne
- Keep a to-do list

Don't

- Try any new treatments or products too close to D-Day. Keep a gap of at least a month before the wedding date.
- Have too many late nights

- Drink too much caffeine and alcohol
- Leave everything to the last minute
- Most importantly, do not wax hair from the face, chest or back as it could lead to a breakout.

The days leading up to the wedding can be very stressful so do take out time and meditate or just sit with your eyes closed for 10-15 minutes everyday to de-stress yourself. You can pray, do your pranayama or whatever it takes to maintain that mental equilibrium. You're getting married. It's an exciting, life-changing event. And it is meant to be enjoyed.

6

Fine Lines

I see it all the time – someone coming in to my consulting room pinching a sagging cheek or holding up a drooping mouth or self-consciously touching the acne on their face. They come in to treat the problems on the surface of the skin because it's affecting the way they feel about themselves inside. I know that when the vitamins, creams, jars, wands, peels or injections have done their job, my clients look noticeably happier, their confidence significantly restored. And that's why I do what I do.

Beautification has always made me happy, right from the time I was a school girl. And I like to see beautification make other people happy as well. If something is bothering you to the point where it's always playing on your mind or is interfering with your day-to-day existence, then why not avail of all that technology has to offer? Isn't that what modern-day discourse is all about? Whether it's what you see in ads, what's being taught in schools, what's being posted on social media, we are always being encouraged to do what makes *us* happy.

Why, then, is there so much *anti*-anti-ageing? Anti-ageing, especially injectibles and surgery, has been surrounded by a culture of silence in India and many of those who inject themselves with Botox or fillers would rather perpetuate that culture. To embrace ageing in its entirety without addressing it at *all* is a debate that is sometimes played out on TV and, at other times, played out within us. I still think that it's a very personal conversation that you need to have with yourself, and whether you should or shouldn't use advanced anti-ageing techniques is entirely up to you. However, in the last part of this book, Fine Lines, I would like to leave you with the thought of growing old gracefully by *anti-ageing* with grace. Because, sometimes, in the removal of fine lines and wrinkles, other lines get crossed.

There's a fine line between looking *too* young and looking *younger*. When I get requests from clients in their fifties who expect anti-ageing treatments to make them look like they are in their thirties, it becomes hard for me sometimes to temper that expectation. You have come in to erase lines. Why would you want to erase the last twenty years of a life lived? In those twenty years, you may have had children, you may have built a business, you may have seen both life and death up close. Why try to wipe out the things that makes you *you*?

One of the world's most prolific anti-ageing superstars, Dr Neil Sadick, puts it beautifully when he says, 'Look good for your decade.' I agree. You can always look beautifully *younger* and good for your age, maybe five or ten years younger. It's very different from looking unrealistically young. When you go out in public, you want to attract compliments like 'good', 'radiant', 'fresh', 'glowing' but you don't want to hear things like 'oh, he or she is trying to look younger' or 'he or she is trying too hard'. The effort to look drastically younger does the exact opposite of what you have set out to achieve; you usually wind up looking like an older person just *trying* to look younger. Look good. For your *decade*.

There's a fine line between transformation and *mutation*. It's not just plastic surgery that can go wrong. Even if they are reversible, so many non-surgical treatments go wrong all the time – heavy-handedness with fillers or Botox, over-insistence by clients who want to make their lips plumper and plumper, unrealistic expectations derived from unrealistic ideals. I've walked away from clients who have been too forceful about injecting more and more fillers. It has to be aesthetically pleasing to my eyes. After a point, even though I know that this is what the client wants, I stop working on them. Less *has* to be more. Because I know what would look good on a client or anyone I'm treating. It's my job.

There's a fine line between loving and hating yourself. This is perhaps the most important distinction of them all: *the difference between positive dissatisfaction and negative dissatisfaction*. If you go to a doctor every few months for touch ups, you are positively dissatisfied in that you are trying to positively enhance your existing self; it is almost like spring cleaning your house on a regular basis. You go when you are dissatisfied but you leave feeling satisfied until the next time you have to touch up.

But when your journey into anti-ageing catapults you into a fault-finding mission that makes you self-critical and plunges you into self-hate, when you start poring over every line, sag and wrinkle, I call this negative dissatisfaction. Because you leave after your treatment thinking *only* of what *next* needs to be sorted. Negative dissatisfaction is when you are *never* satisfied. Something that was supposed to have made you happy is making you feel worse.

There's never a time that is too late to delay the process of ageing and make those wrinkles wait a little. You can start now, immediately, after you've read the last sentence of this book. But you have to always remember why you are doing it in the first place: *to make yourself happy.* Embrace your decade. Love yourself. Because even when you use the most sophisticated anti-ageing treatments that exist, without self-acceptance and self-love they are of no use. This book may have been packed with tips about age-defying techniques but this, this last part, is the best advice I can ever give you.

7

Beauty Calendars

Daily habits are some of the hardest things to change. To get the full benefit of this book and to give you a ready blueprint which you can use to catapult your journey into new anti-ageing habits, I thought it would be useful, as a parting shot, to design beauty calendars based on the decade you fall into, that is, twenties, thirties, forties and so on. Here are some calendars for daily, weekly and monthly skincare that I believe encapsulate the essential bare minimum you need to put up a fight against ageing. But it's only the bare minimum because I've only listed daily skincare and suggestions for exfoliation and skin tightening. Whether you want to get injected with Botox, get some fillers done or feel that your face would be greatly enhanced by the other techniques mentioned in this book is entirely your prerogative with the hope that you will always do things that make you happy.

20s

Frequency	Procedure	Approximate Time Taken
Daily	**Morning** | Lime Shot, Green Juice, Cleansing, Moisturizing (3 minutes) **Day** | Sunscreen Application and Reapplication (1-2 minutes) **Night** | Cleansing, Make-up Removal, Night Cream [post age 25] (5 minutes)	10-11 minutes
Once in 7-10 Days	Superficial or Mechanical Exfoliation	10 minutes
Once a Month	Medium-Depth or Salon Exfoliation	1 hour

30s

Frequency	Procedure	Approximate Time Taken
Daily	**Morning** | Lime Shot, Green Juice, Cleansing, Moisturizing (3 minutes) **Day** | Sunscreen Application and Reapplication (1-2 minutes) **Night** | Cleansing, Make-up Removal, Night Cream (5 minutes)	10-11 minutes
Once in 7-10 Days	Superficial or Mechanical Exfoliation	10 minutes
Once a Month	Medium-Depth or Salon Exfoliation	1 hour
Once in 6 Months	Deep Exfoliation	Depends on the procedure

40s

Frequency	Procedure	Approximate Time Taken
Daily	**Morning** | Lime Shot, Green Juice, Cleansing, Moisturizing (3 minutes) **Day** | Sunscreen Application and Reapplication (1-2 minutes) **Night** | Cleansing, Make-up Removal, Night Cream (5 minutes)	10-11 minutes
Once in 7-10 Days	Superficial or Mechanical Exfoliation	10 minutes
Once a Month	Medium-Depth or Salon Exfoliation	1 hour
Once in 6 Months	Deep Exfoliation	Depends on the procedure

50s

Frequency	Procedure	Approximate Time Taken
Daily	**Morning** | Lime Shot, Green Juice, Cleansing, Moisturizing (3 minutes) **Day** | Sunscreen Application and Reapplication (1-2 minutes) **Night** | Cleansing, Make-up Removal, Night Cream (5 minutes)	10-11 minutes
Once in 7-10 Days	Superficial or Mechanical Exfoliation	10 minutes
Once a Month	Medium-Depth or Salon Exfoliation	1 hour

Frequency	Procedure	Approximate Time Taken
Once in 6 Months	Deep Exfoliation	Depends on the procedure
Once a Year	Skin Tightening	Depends on the procedure

60+

Frequency	Procedure	Approximate Time Taken
Daily	**Morning** | Lime Shot, Green Juice, Cleansing, Moisturizing (3 minutes) **Day** | Sunscreen Application and Reapplication (1-2 minutes) **Night** | Cleansing, Make-up Removal, Night Cream (5 minutes)	10-11 minutes
Once in 7-10 Days	Superficial or Mechanical Exfoliation	10 minutes
Once a Month	Medium-Depth or Salon Exfoliation	1 hour
Once in 6 Months	Deep Exfoliation	Depends on the procedure
Once a Year	Skin Tightening	Depends on the procedure

Everyone Has to Know

No One Has to Know would have remained an unfulfilled dream but for those who have worked behind the scenes to be present when I was absent during my time spent with this book. Over the last twenty years, so many people have contributed both directly and indirectly to this work, which is why I would like everyone to know how much I owe to:

My kids Gaurav, Ashwin, Chaitra and Mihika and my little grandson Aryan for making sacrifices to be there for me.

Mihika, who helped me navigate this book through what sounded right and what didn't.

Ashwin, whose sharp mind helped me build Blush into what it is today.

My parents and my mother-in-law, without whom it would have been impossible to follow my heart. And my dreams.

Mrs Kokilaben Ambani, who has always been a source of unstinting support. Thank you for considering me a part of your family.

My cockerspaniel Cuddles for all the emotional support. And the cuddles.

The Times Group, who I have been closely associated with for the last twenty years.

The Miss India Organization for believing in me and putting that little tiara on Blush, enhancing its association with glamour and beauty.

The Press, whose support I enjoy both nationally and internationally.

Pradeep Guha, who spotted my potential and kick-started my association with *Femina* and Miss India. Thank you, Pradeep. You started it all.

Amy Fernandes, whose first article on my work twenty years ago put Blush on the fast track to success.

Sathya Saran, former editor of *Femina*. I will always cherish the special moments we have shared, and continue to.

John Abraham, Mandira Bedi, Juhi Chawla, Diana Hayden and Pooja Chopra, who have been there for me anytime, anywhere. God bless you.

Rashmi Uday Singh, my dearest friend. I will never forget your relentless efforts over the past fifteen years towards making me write this book.

Rita Dhody, my sweetest friend, who I credit for my bringing Botox to India, among many, many other things.

Vikram and Jaya Tannan, who have been my guiding lights both personally and professionally for the past twenty years.

My close friends Suchi, Shashi and Shaila. You've been there for me in more ways than you can imagine.

My invaluable team at my clinics and franchises including doctors, specialists, technicians, front office and back office staff, without whom there would be no Blush.

Gayatri Pahlajani, my writer, whose dedication and creativity has made this book what it is.

Dr Asma Patel, associate doctor at Blush and my assistant on this book, without whom the book would probably have taken another two years. Thank you so much.

Karthika V.K., the enigmatic editor-in-chief of HarperCollins India, whose encouragement further propelled me to write this book.

Debasri Rakshit, my editor at HarperCollins India, whose painstaking eye has strengthened my voice.

Jojy Philip, the typesetter, for his incredible commitment to laying out this book.

And finally, to my loyal and fantastically supportive clients, especially to those who sent in testimonials. Thank you for believing in me and for spreading the word. Your warm, unquestionable faith in me makes *me* blush.

I thank you all.